Counting People In

Changing the way we think about membership and the Church

Richard Thomas

First published in Great Britain in 2003 by
Society for Promoting Christian Knowledge
Holy Trinity Church
Marylebone Road
London NW1 4DU

British Library Cataloguing-in-Publication Data
A catalogue record for this book is available from the British Library

ISBN 0–281–05397–9

1 3 5 7 9 10 8 6 4 2

Typeset by Wilmaset, Merseyside, Wirral
Printed in Great Britain by
The Cromwell Press, Trowbridge, Wiltshire

Contents

Introduction

This book is about belonging. Specifically, it is about changes in the way
in which people belong to the Church in our changing culture, and about
the barriers to belonging that are raised by both the way we organize the
Church and the way we try to organize belief. Its aim is to contribute to the
discussion about how Christian faith and discipleship can be developed in
a rapidly changing culture where identity is formed not so much by participative memberships, but by association with brands and issues, by
information and by the understanding of spirituality gained through the
print and broadcast media. In particular, it aims to develop an evangelistic
strategy that takes us away from a narrow, cult-like expression of membership towards a celebration of Christianity which sees the world, rather
than the Church, as a sacred place, the place where the gospel is discovered,
and where many more people can engage with the dynamic of Christian
faith and discipleship.

In her book *Religion in Britain since 1945*, sociologist Grace Davie uses
the phrase 'believing without belonging'. From a sociological perspective
she started a debate that has developed into deeper theological reflection.
Her assumption, implicit in the phrase itself, is that believing and belonging are different things, and that somehow belief without belonging is
incomplete. This book takes a different approach. It accepts, perhaps
critically, that from a sociological perspective it is useful to separate
belief from belonging, and that this approach is necessary in order to
describe the phenomenon. But while it may serve a sociological
methodology, the idea that belonging somehow authenticates belief is
theologically inadequate. This book will argue that, from a theological
perspective, belief is in itself a kind of belonging, perhaps even the
strongest, most potent form of belonging.

I will argue that today's Church has two kinds of members. There are
those who form the core of our worshipping communities, who participate – if not Sunday by Sunday, at least for a majority of Sundays – in
regular worship, join house groups, and maintain the fabric of the organ-

v

ization. And then there are those who still feel strongly that they belong, but who rarely participate in the organized life of the Church. These are people who 'associate' themselves with Christianity, even if their theology might be unformed or decidedly 'fuzzy'; people who rarely participate but who, if asked whether they belong to a church, would strongly affirm their 'membership'. In a Gallup poll conducted in the autumn of 1996 as part of the Church's preparation for the millennium celebrations, 54 per cent of the population made this claim for themselves. We will define this group as 'associate members', or those who belong by association, rather than by participation.

Of course, the boundary between participant members and those who belong by association is not sharp, nor is it always easily discernible. The one kind of membership flows into the other without clear distinctions at the edges. And the boundary is not an impermeable barrier: participant members may take time out for a host of reasons, and associate members may opt into participation for shorter or longer periods of time. There is a degree of crossover that creates pitfalls for any attempt to classify the process.

The attitude of the Church's participant members to those who belong by association, and therefore the attitude of the institution itself, has traditionally been to see them as 'fringe' members, a potentially fruitful market for evangelization. The purpose of much of this evangelism has been to try to turn them into regular participant members: put crudely, to get them into the Church and to keep them there. Yet the experience of the decade of evangelism, and of most evangelistic enterprises since about 1980, has been that this simply doesn't work. This book will argue that this approach is not merely unproductive, but actually counter-productive to the mission of the Church. Despite the apparent success of the Alpha Courses and the growth of the culture of certainty, the overall number of participant members in most churches, and certainly in the Church of England, continues to decline. Alongside this continuing slow decline, there has been a massive growth of interest in what many people call 'self-defining' spirituality. Secularism has imploded and spirituality has re-emerged as one of the key issues of a postmodern society. Yet in a society where institutional religion is regarded with suspicion if not outright hostility, the churches have been unable to take the risk of changing their structures in ways sufficiently radical to embrace this new and exciting challenge.

The way in which people belong to organizations, including the churches, has changed radically, but we are still largely a church that only values its participant members. For example, more than 90 per cent of our budget is spent on developing the faith and discipleship of the 8 per cent of the population who regularly come to church, but only a very small fraction is spent, often accidentally, on developing the faith of the 35 per cent of the population who belong by association. The success of the television cartoon series *Story-Keepers* is a significant example of how the transmission of the gospel stories to this group of people has shifted from the Church to the media, yet the churches scarcely appear to have noticed the significance of this audience. We need to embrace the changes in culture that have happened before our very eyes, changes that most of us have willingly participated in, and demonstrate the same confidence and faith in those around us as Jesus did when he went out into the streets and marketplaces with the good news of God's love, healing and forgiveness. He didn't give his life on the cross merely to turn us into regular churchgoers; he gave his life that everyone might have a life-transforming relationship with God himself. The organized churches might not find the idea easy or comforting, but the possibility of such a relationship for people who are not regular participants is not merely real, but a central challenge to our evangelism. Finding ways of speaking to the spirituality of a generation who do not come to church is not a matter of bringing them in, but of changing our understanding of the nature of the Church itself.

Chapter 1

Belonging in an Age of Unbelonging

Rationalism, Mechanics and the Search for Spirituality

One of the features of our rational society is the search for causes. Our scientific analysis is based on cause and effect: we see the effects, and attempt to discover the causes for them. The world is viewed as a machine, and any problem with its operation is seen as a fault that can be corrected once the machine is fully understood. But such a mechanistic approach tends to exclude any sense of the transcendent; God is seen simply as a way of explaining the bits of the machine that we do not yet fully understand. In a similar way, a large part of our theological reflection over the past fifty years or so has been driven by the same underlying desire to explain our beliefs in terms of their causes. Some have argued that this approach has simply echoed the secular rationalism that has deconstructed any sense of the sacred or the transcendent, and by so doing has reinforced the rationalization of religious belief.[1] The 'Honest to God' debate of the seventies is a good example of this process. Many would argue that we have been starved of spirituality, of a sense of the sacred, by the very institutions to which we have looked to satisfy our hunger: that we are searching for communities where the transcendent is not only recognized, but where the sacredness of being rather than its rationality is the starting point.

But in order to understand the dilemma facing the churches, and to regain the confidence to move from what is basically a rationalist, even secularist, understanding of Christianity to a spirituality that is much deeper and more satisfying, we need to understand something at least of the context of the problem.

Most thoughtful Christians would agree that our national culture has changed dramatically over the past fifty years. One of the effects of the Thatcherite era was the development of a 'contract culture' where stability was seen as an enemy of progress, and people were hired, and fired, according to the needs of the machine. The consequent change in work patterns for both men and women has been huge. No longer do you join a company on leaving school or university and expect to remain in it until retirement. Not only are you likely to change your employer much more frequently; you are also likely to have to change the skills for which you are employed. Families where both father and mother go to work are the norm, rather than the exception. The result of this change alone is that 'family time' is under pressure. No longer is there a pool of people ready to take part in voluntary activities; we have learned to 'buy in' those things that we need for ourselves. Rather than a community of contributors, we are a nation of consumers where the answer to all our problems is to be found in our ability to purchase the solutions. Even our caring has been secularized; we talk in terms of resources for social services, hospitals, childcare, and a host of other 'services' where people operate like the repair mechanics for an increasingly creaky machine. There is little time or mental landscape for mystery, for contemplation or prayer. Instead of looking beyond ourselves to the energy that gives us life, we look inside ourselves for the mechanics of living.

The change in Sunday trading laws was an almost inevitable consequence of this process. If there ever was a national sense of the 'sacredness' of Sunday, even as the day when we 'ought' to go to church but don't, it has finally disappeared for all but a minority of Christians. For the majority of the population, shopping and leisure activities have largely taken the place of keeping the Sabbath 'holy'. Most churchgoers will happily attend a Sunday morning service, and then go straight round to the local supermarket to do the shopping, stopping off on the way to collect the children from the local football club, the gym or the swimming pool. For most Christians at the beginning of the twenty-first century, there are only nine commandments; the fourth commandment has withered on the vine. Even the arguments of the 'Keep Sunday Special' campaign have colluded with this consumerism, which is itself a product of the mechanization of our world-view. We are told that we need to preserve the special nature of Sunday in order for families to have time together. But time for what? For shared leisure, shared consumption? In a secularized and mechanistic world, even churchgoing is presented in terms of a mechanical solution to the flaws in the social machine. We go to church for fuel to keep the spiritual machine running, then to the shops for food for the physical machine. Yet the most fundamental reason for keeping Sunday 'special' is that it reflects the sacred, and helps us as a community to keep the sacred at the heart of our common life.

Media and Shared Identity

At the same time, we have seen an expansion in media and communications technology that has led to changes as great as those of the industrial revolution. The print and broadcast media have increasingly created a cohesive sense of identity across England, Scotland and Wales, and with it the possibility of national expressions of grief or celebration, with their associated spirituality, that were not possible in previous generations. Writing in 1994, shortly after the Hillsborough tragedy, when 94 people were crushed to death at the start of a football match in the Anfield stadium in Liverpool, Grace Davie says:

> What started as a series of spontaneous actions by individual mourners (the laying of flowers on the pitch, for example) became within twenty-four hours a shared or communal activity. The Anfield Pilgrimage expressed, indeed enacted, the mood of an entire city, a city united in grief, an example surely of effective civic religion. To what extent might this episode become typical of British behaviour or will Liverpool – in this as in other ways – remain the exception rather than the norm? . . . I have argued elsewhere . . . that what happened at Anfield depended very considerably on the prior existence of Liverpool's exceptionally strong communal identity. For this reason, such an explicit, conscious and collective acknowledgement of death is, I think, unlikely to be repeated. It is a special case. (Davie 1994: 91)

Davie was writing before the events of August 1997, when the sudden and tragic death of the Princess of Wales was followed by a massive national act of mourning. The central role of the media in providing a cohesive and almost universal sense of common ritual again took the nation by surprise. But the media were not creating the response; at times they found it difficult to keep up with it. That the identifiable rituals should include the placing of flowers, the lighting of candles, and acts of pilgrimage only shows that Davie is right to identify strong elements of active Christian spirituality in what she calls 'common religion'. With over 75 per cent of the population cremated after death, either with or following a (more or less) Christian act of worship, where candles and flowers are perhaps the most potent and accessible symbols, it is little wonder that we are conditioned to use these same symbols in our common acts of grieving. The massive public response to the death of Princess Diana was probably the first time that this was widely recognized; we became a single community, sharing similar rituals of grief, bound together by the unifying narrative brought to us through television, radio and newspapers, drawing on the symbols of our crematorium culture.

Yet not everyone felt they could identify with this supposedly common experience. There was an identifiable group who rejected the media hype, and the construct of a nation united in a spiritual act of mourning. They felt untouched by the death of the Princess, and alienated by the ritual.

In a similar way, the fuel tax protests in September 2000 showed how a sense of common grievance could be shared through the media; ordinary, sensible, courteous people engaged in a protest that, according to the media, had huge popular support. There was a sense of solidarity in the situation that contrasted sharply with the 'them and us' atmosphere of earlier strikes and protests. Yet once again, there was an identifiable group of people who did not share the media's perceptions.

We are increasingly getting a sense of identity and shared concerns through the print, and particularly the broadcast, media. But that media perception, though powerful, is itself more about theatre than about reality, and may be as much a function of editorial fantasy as it is of national fact. We create theatre not only to entertain, but also to convince. When a television producer frames the shots in order to get maximum visual impact, she necessarily rejects other interpretations. She is making a choice in order to convey a message to the viewer. And because it is good theatre, full of colour and sound and energy and emotion, and because we share the same stage and recognize the backdrops, we can easily be convinced that this theatre is reality. In these great national dramas, we become part of the cast, and play our part in whatever way the directors suggest. We join the cast of thousands in laying flowers at the place of tragedy, or in wearing red noses to raise money for children in need. Drawn into this world of theatre, it is easy to lose any sense of the boundary between reality and fiction. Tabloid newspapers report the events of television soaps alongside the floods in south India as though both were happening in the 'real world'. The emphases are not false, in the sense that they are wrong; but they are partial, in the sense that they convey only one aspect of a much more complex reality.

And along with the drama, we are subtly invited to share the theological preconceptions of the media. Anyone who has worked in a newsroom of one of our major media outlets will recognize the secular fundamentalism that drives most of its thinking. For journalists, there can be no God because nothing is sacred. No one is without sin, and it is the task of the journalist to expose that sin so that its perpetrators can be properly excommunicated. Thus the great institutions of our nation, the monarchy, Parliament, the churches, all come under attack. The moment human failure is identified, it is publicized in order that the reader, the listener or the viewer may see for him- or herself the need for purification. Editors clamour for the resignation of politicians, the naming and shaming of paedophiles, or the abdication of princes – whatever it takes to purge the nation. Like all forms of fundamentalism, it is not about forgiveness and restoration, but about accusation, excommunication and the preservation of purity. And it is a natural result of a mechanistic view of the world, where failure or wrongdoing is seen as a weakness in the machine rather than an opportunity to forgive and to grow.

Disintermediation – Going Direct!

'Disintermediation' is one of the buzzwords of the Internet, and particularly the banking and insurance sectors. It means the removal of the intermediary. 'Cutting out the middleman' was originally a profit-driven concept, but it is increasingly seen in terms of putting the producer of goods or services directly in touch with the customer. First in insurance, then in banking, we have seen the telephone take the place of the local branch or insurance broker. Financial institutions have seen many of their traditional customers drift away to businesses that trade directly with the public by telephone or direct mail. Travel agencies are another area where people go direct; teletext and Internet sales combine to squeeze out the local travel shop.

At first sight, this process looks like a direct result of the search for value. If I can get my holiday, or my insurance, or my furniture direct from the manufacturer, I can add value to the product by getting it cheaper. But there is something deeper than financial gain which is driving the progress of disintermediation. By going direct, I can be sure of authenticity. The product will not have gone through so many different hands; it will somehow be purer, more authentic. The logical outcome of this assumption that one gets greater authenticity by 'going direct to the manufacturer' is the mistrust and ultimate rejection of the intermediary. If the intermediary adds a percentage to the cost, he can also dilute the product. And so all intermediaries are suspect.

And the churches are excellent examples of intermediaries for which there is cause for suspicion in precisely these two areas. There is a cost in belonging to an institutional church. Not only are there financial demands in maintaining the institution as an institution, but there is a cost in time and energy simply in going to the services and meetings. Yet if membership of the Church is primarily about belief (and certainly the churches have sold themselves in this way for many years) then the principle of disintermediation suggests that belief can be held and practised more efficiently without the added cost of church membership.

Of course, membership of a community of faith may be primarily about sharing the same beliefs, but it is not exclusively about belief. It is about the way we live the lifestyle of the Kingdom, which is both eucharistic in the sense that it is about the quality and richness of the life we live together, and sacrificial in the sense that we live for each other under God, rather than for ourselves. Ironically, the one thing that has apparently been so successful in attracting participants – the Alpha Course and its derivatives – itself reinforces the view that Christianity is about living a particular belief; and if Christianity is primarily about belief, that raises real doubts about the necessity of participation in the local church except as a school from which graduation is inevitable at some unspecified point in the future. There is also the sense, present especially in regular church members, that the institutional church is diluting the product. It is a common, if not often expressed, feeling amongst many churchgoers that 'there must be more to Christianity than this'.

So where the institutional churches are perceived not only to be adding a percentage to Christian discipleship, but also to be diluting the product, it is not long before the consumer 'goes direct'. The authenticity of a poorly mediated faith is called into question by the experience of the worshipper, who longs for a deeper and more meaningful spirituality.

Belonging as 'Choice'

One of my parishioners living in an urban council estate in the mid-1980s put a sign up in his front garden. It read: 'You are nearer to God in the garden than anywhere else on earth.' And of course, in many ways he was right. The record of our Christian journey doesn't start with our entry into a church building, but with the great drama of creation, where God brings matter into being and makes it pregnant with purpose and meaning, with life and energy, and ultimately with the life of his Spirit. A Christianity that sees the sacred merely in terms of what happens within a special building is a seriously deficient faith. As we shall see in more detail a little later, the rise of ecological awareness has led to a recognition of the spiritual nature of our world in those who have little or no Christian background, and has led our worship on a journey outside the confines of the church building.

Our perception about the change in the way people 'belong' to the Church is underlined by changes in the way people belong to other organizations and institutions. To give a fairly simple example, the way that people make their decision about how to vote in a political election has changed remarkably. Even as late as the 1950s, people would go along to the local village or town hall to hear the candidates speak. They would make up their minds, or at least confirm their prejudices, through personal contact. Membership of the political parties was strong. But at the beginning of the new millennium, actual card-carrying membership of all the political parties has declined sharply. It is rare for anyone other than party activists to go to political meetings or election hustings. Most people get their information largely from the print and broadcast media, and make up their mind how to vote on the basis of the media coverage. But ask any of them which party they 'belong' to, and they will probably still have a fairly clear idea. They may have switched allegiance, but there will still be an allegiance, a form of 'belonging', that is as strong as it always was. Only the nature of that 'belonging' will have changed. They will be unlikely to be card-carrying members any more. They will not be 'participants', but 'associates'. But they will feel that they 'belong' no less than their parents did in a previous generation. Compared with the political parties, the Church of England along with most other churches has been remarkably successful in maintaining a participant membership. But unlike the political parties and some highly successful organizations, we have failed to recognize the changes for what they are, and have tended to concentrate solely on maintaining participation. The result is that we have alienated those people who feel that they still belong to the Church as much as they ever did, but who now relate in a different way, and we are in danger of wasting an enormous opportunity.

This distinction between participation and association is central to an understanding of belonging. The two words 'participation' and 'association' are not in themselves definitive, but they will more or less bear the weight of the argument. To be a participant member is to take part in the structural, or institutional, life of the organization. It is to have signed up; it is to give time and energy, and usually money, to the support of the institution or organization that embodies the beliefs. And here is the clue to the rejection of the institution, to the disintermediation of Christianity. People are not interested in supporting institutions or organizations as ends in themselves. They are not happy for their money to be used to pay for what is increasingly perceived as the bureaucracy of the Church, nor for their time and energy to be spent running it. Or at least, they need to have a clear and convincing case put to them as to why their money and energy should be used in this way.

To be an associate member is perceived as having the beliefs of Christianity without dilution; it is perceived as liberating limited finances to help the poor rather than perpetuate the institutional bureaucracy, and as using time efficiently to create quality relationships within the family or local community without the additional burden that participant membership involves.

Mobility has also played a part, albeit a smaller one, in this change in the way we relate to each other. Moving house has been recognized as one of the major causes for people 'losing touch' with the Church. Relationships take time to build. The energy needed to locate a new church, set aside a regular time to worship, and build new relationships, often in the context of a different, possibly uncomfortable theology or spirituality, is hard to find if you are also coping with a new job, a new house, commuting, and growing children who probably prefer the football club to church worship.

For all these reasons, and for many others, the way in which we belong to things has changed. Increasingly, we identify with brands and ideas, rather than groups and meetings. We espouse causes, often carefully branded and marketed to enable us to support them without requiring our participation in the organizations themselves. Our sense of identity is shaped more by the brands and causes we support than by the meetings or clubs we belong to. Leisure, fitness and spirituality are at the top of the list when it comes to popular aspirations (Henley Centre research, 1999) yet the churches have missed this fundamental change in perception and continue to fret about declining participation, or worse, attempt to massage the figures that demonstrate this change in order to avoid the challenge of having to change themselves.

Crisis or Spiritual Search?

For any organization structured around 'joining', these changes in our culture pose problems. At an organizational level there will be issues such as funding and resources; for an organization tied to participant membership, empty seats mean a shrinking funding base and questions about deployment. At an educational level, it means a decline in the number of people who can relate to the narratives of the organization – fewer people who understand the language or remember the stories. And for a Church that has centred its whole life around participative worship, it can appear as a crisis of faith in a secular nation. Media stories about the Church are increasingly prefaced by the misleading and discouraging words 'in these days of declining church congregations', while we urge ourselves to undertake yet more 'evangelism', by which we mean the offering of dogmatic statements that we hope will lead to recruitment into participant membership.

Yet these cultural changes are not necessarily unhelpful to the Christian mission. Greater mobility, changes in the pattern of work and leisure, shifts in family identity, the primacy of the media as the framework for our world-view, and the growth of the Internet all contribute to this changing approach to 'belonging'. For many people inside the Church this change is interpreted as decline, while the organization of the Church exclusively in terms of participation in local worshipping communities is becoming a barrier to an increasing number of people who relate in other ways. But such a negative view of the life of the spirit fails to account for the huge numbers of young people who travel each year to Taizé, or who make the journey to Iona; it fails to account for the rapid growth in alternative spiritualities; it fails to recognize the 180-degree shift in direction whereby people look to the Church as a resource for their own spirituality, rather than allow the Church to use them as a resource for its own needs.

It is too easy to blame the secularization of our culture for this apparent decline in participative membership. This was the accepted diagnosis of the sixties and early seventies. But by any measure of the evidence, our culture is by no means secular. The Henley Centre research showed that in 1999, 20 per cent of the population wanted to make changes in their spirituality, 27 per cent had successfully made changes, and 3 per cent had tried but failed. A massive 50 per cent of the population was engaged in practical action with regard to their own spirituality in the year leading up to the millennium celebrations! It is not God that is dead; secularism is dead, or at least in terminal decline. Postmodernism has given way to post-secularism, where the meta-narrative of the absence of any kind of transcendent values or beliefs has given way to a kind of spiritual pluralism in which Christianity is enhanced by the counterpoint of other world religions, including the rise of the new paganism.

This deep spiritual dissatisfaction with much of our materialistic individualism, both personally and organizationally, is accompanied by a new freedom and acceptance for different faiths and spiritualities. Much of this has flowed from the new emphasis on the environment; countless school assemblies promoting the saving of whales and dolphins, the recycling of paper and glass, and other ways of caring for the environment have bred in us a growing awareness of the centrality of nature for our well-being. Such an awareness takes us out of our narrow materialism, and points to something beyond us – something bigger and greater than ourselves. Such a journey of awareness leads naturally to the recognition of the divine, or at least the immanence of the spirit, in nature. A spirituality that does not make connections with the soil and leaf of creation, that does not see us as part of a created order which is itself a spiritual phenomenon, indeed a fundamental expression of God, will not attract. It is no accident that the new paganism, with its spirituality centred on place and nature, is one of the fastest-growing religions in the UK. But in the secular world of politics, economics and science, it comes as a severe shock that the ecological movement of the seventies and eighties has given birth to a world-view that views the transcendence and immanence of the divine as perhaps the single most important measure of right and wrong. While the road protests of the late nineties, with their tree-huggers and their diggers, were seen by the media within their own secular terms of ecological protest, the protesters themselves often defined their protests in terms of their spirituality; they were engaged in a spiritual struggle for the land. For many of them, Goddess worship – recognizing the sacred nature of the landscape – was a major, if not the central, driving force behind their actions.

Another important factor in the way we belong to organizations is the change in our attitude to authority. Contemporary educational practice encourages us all to question received authority. It is essentially experiential; it starts with our own experience and builds empirically on that. No longer do we sit in neat rows being taught to accept what our teachers claim to believe. We are encouraged to begin with our own experience, and to develop our own understanding of how things are. For a Church that holds to the importance of a revelation received from God, this approach poses its own challenges. Dogmatic assertions are rejected in favour of personal experience. In today's culture, where people trust their own experience first and are uneasy about being told what to believe, evangelism itself, or at least evangelism in the way that many of us experienced it, may well have become not simply unproductive, but counter-productive.

'Churn' and the Problem of Retention

So despite a much-publicized 'decade of evangelism', church attendance in England appears to have declined faster than in almost any other country, while at the same time we have witnessed a rapid growth in 'green' spiritualities. A hostile and cynical media increasingly deals blows to confidence in the Church's task. We are increasingly failing to connect with people. And even the most committed Christians, lay and ordained, have begun openly to question whether the Church has somehow got it wrong.

But is this analysis entirely correct? After all, it is claimed that the most rapidly growing sector of the Church is precisely that sector which is the most dogmatic. People, we are told, want straightforward answers to life's questions. Those churches that claim to give simple, unambiguous answers seem to be growing rapidly. But even this apparently clear indication of spiritual need is not what it might at first seem. While it is true that such churches attract a higher proportion of participant members, their retention rate is questionable. The search for personal meaning in a world where the levels of uncertainty and change are high initially attracts people to churches where dogmatic certainty is the norm. But there is a high turnover rate – what in the broadcast industry is called 'churn'.

The same thing can be seen in the satellite television industry. Large numbers of people are attracted to the offer of films or sport on demand, and sign up for the dish on the side of the house. They try it for a year, perhaps two years, but then find the cost of the subscription is no longer balanced by the satisfaction gained from the little square box, and they let the subscription lapse. The consequence is that, despite considerable numbers of people signing up for satellite television each year, the industry finds it very hard to increase its penetration beyond 15 per cent of the population. Anyone who has had satellite television and has allowed the subscription to lapse will know only too well that the companies put a lot of resources into trying to persuade you to return. Initial membership is not the issue; the key issue is retention. Unless they can keep the members they attract, they will not develop their brand or increase their market share.

In the longer term, 'churn', whether it be in satellite television or in church membership, is highly counter-productive. It is much easier to attract those who have had no experience of satellite television than it is to bring back those who have allowed their subscription to lapse. In much the same way, it is difficult to bring back to church those who have tried it once and found it lacking in longer-term spiritual or intellectual satisfaction.

The Progression from Simplicity to Wisdom

A close examination of those churches that are not only growing, but also retaining participant members, would almost certainly show that there are two key factors at work. The first is how they manage the progression from simplicity, through complexity, towards clarity and truth. When you know little or nothing about a subject, it is relatively easy to be attracted by clear, simple statements that seem convincing. But as you learn more, so the issues become increasingly complex, and the solutions you initially thought were so convincing begin to appear less satisfactory. There usually follows a period of complexity, even confusion, in which a great deal of work needs to be done in sorting out a more complex, though often more satisfying, solution. In terms of Christian discipleship, the period of complexity and possible confusion can last a long time, because there is often a great deal of sorting out to do. But the other side of complexity is clarity, and it is to this clarity – or to use the language of the Old Testament, to this wisdom – that we are called.

So the progression from simplicity, through complexity, to clarity or wisdom is a vital process, and people need to be supported and encouraged through an important period of personal, theological and spiritual growth. Sadly, what so often happens is that as church members begin to address their faith, they begin to find themselves in transition from simplicity to complexity. A key part of the sorting out is to look beyond the simple answers to try to find a more satisfying solution: sometimes, even, to look outside the church to other spiritualities or faiths. To their house-group leader, to inexperienced clergy or church leaders, and often to the individuals themselves, it can appear that they are 'losing their faith', when in reality they are merely deepening it. The response of some church leaders is to exhort them to hold on to the simple, or simplistic, answers that first attracted them. But this is fatal to retention: people will be torn between loyalty to the church that has supported them, sometimes through crises in their lives, and loyalty to their own integrity as their understanding of Christian faith expands. The tension can only be maintained for a while. They either grow, or leave.

Social Engagement and a Return to Spirituality

The second issue is that of social engagement. The church that encourages its members not only to believe certain things, but to put those beliefs into practice, is the church that will both attract and retain members. Research into the reasons why people leave churches has shown that they become bored and disillusioned when they are unable to see practical applications for their new faith (Richter and Francis 1998). In many of the growing churches, as people enter the confusion that develops as they progress from simplicity to complexity, they are encouraged to put their faith to practical use. Practical action 'earths' or roots them in reality, and gives them an anchor for a changing understanding of God or Christianity that would otherwise threaten their belonging. Many of the growing churches are growing not because they present a simplistic theology, but because they engage with the social and practical concerns of their members and the communities within which they worship. Such engagement does not allow any false simplicity; the complexities of faith in action very quickly move people forward, and at the same time provide a framework of action that creates a secure environment for growth.

The Church, and particularly the Church of England, appears to be facing a crisis of membership. It is not that people are no longer attracted to spiritual issues, or that spirituality is dead; nearly all the relevant research shows us that people are increasingly discovering the spiritual dimension of their lives and wanting to explore it. It is that we have failed to listen to, and therefore to understand, the aspirations of people who are suddenly rediscovering their spirituality. The secular culture has given way to the multiplex culture, where you can choose your own world-view, and where many world-views rub shoulders with each other. The very nature of the multiplex leads from the secular to the transcendent simply because it points away from a single world-view to the possibility of the 'other'; spirituality is once again a real option in a society that recognizes the truth that life without transcendent values is both dangerous and dull.

The institutional churches have concentrated on participant membership to the exclusion of nearly everything else. They have abandoned, and have appeared to alienate, not only those who still feel that they belong but also those who may want to rejoin a community where transcendent spiritual values and experience are central. We have concentrated on doctrine and church politics to the exclusion of practical action, leaving action and new ways of thinking to the para-church societies and mission organizations. We have drawn tight doctrinal boundaries, created what is almost a 'cult of Jesus' where the overarching belief in the God of creation has given way to the promotion of a divine cult-leader, one who apparently calls his followers to disengage from the world and to give money to support the cult rather than the poor, and who offers a message of exclusion rather than inclusion. We have tended to behave more and more like a cult, at first neglecting, then blaming, the growing number of people who belong by association. Yet these 'associate' members are the key to a proper understanding of our mission.

Chapter 2

Belonging: Defining the Terms

Participation and Association

The first hypothesis of this book, put simply, is that believing is belonging, and possibly the strongest form of belonging. The second is that the Church has two kinds of members. There are those who belong by participating in the organized life of a church. They come, reasonably regularly, to worship. They take part in house groups. They are members of the parochial church council, or help with any number of things that contribute to the structural life of the church. For want of a better word, we have called them 'participants'. Their faith is formed and developed through their participation in the local church; they form the basis for 'membership' figures, and on them falls the largest part of the burden of funding the mission of the Church. And the evidence from most, if not all, of the statistical surveys is that as a proportion of the population their numbers are steadily declining.

Then there are those who may not come, even irregularly, to worship. They will not be found on the lists of those who take part in house groups, or as members of parochial church councils. But if asked, they will state quite firmly that they belong. This sense of belonging might be expressed as a claim to be a member of the Church of England, or the Catholic Church, or some other Christian tradition. These are people who belong by association, rather than by participation. We will avoid the term 'affiliation' because the same word was used extensively, with a broader meaning, by the sociologist of religion, Émile Durkheim.

Both these groups, broadly defined, are essential to the development of a sense of Christian sacredness in our culture. We need strong, open and theologically aware communities to maintain Christian worship, challenge the emptiness of a secular mindset, and provide a core group of people who can model the contemporary equivalent of Jesus' disciples. Most of all, we desperately need these communities to be open to serve those who belong by association, and to provide a contact point for those who have no sense of belonging, but who have just begun to recognize the emptiness of a life that is not centred on God. The problem is that many of these communities have seen themselves, or have been taught to see themselves, as closed communities, whose purpose is to be like plants in a greenhouse, whose growth is an end in itself. I will argue later that one fruitful model for thinking about the contemporary Christian congregation is that of the monastery. The congregation exists to create a microcosm of the Kingdom of God, to develop a sense of community life lived in obedience to God and in support of its individual members, to act out the life of the spirit within a particular geographical and human context. But like the monasteries, its primary purpose lies outside itself. Its Christian mission is not simply to gather more members into the enclosed life, but to provide a centre for Christian spirituality at the heart of the community within which it is set. It is there for the education, support, healing and care of that wider community. In contemporary language, it needs to be open and transparent, infinitely supportive of those who belong by association.

We have seen in the previous chapter that belonging by association is a phenomenon that is not confined to the churches. Increasingly, for example, political parties are having to come to terms with the shift in belonging from participation towards association. Ask any random sample of people about their political affiliation, and a significant number will express a sense of belonging that strongly identifies with one or other of the political parties. 'I'm Labour' or 'I'm Tory' does not mean that they are paid-up participant, card-carrying members of the local party. It may mean, and is increasingly likely to mean, that they belong by association, rather than participation.

But how can we measure the two groups of people – those who belong to the Church by participation, and those who belong by association? First, the boundary between the two groups is not clearly defined, and second, the statistical evidence is far from easy to interpret.

Measuring Membership

Durkheim defines religious activity in terms of affiliation, practice and belief. And rather unhelpfully for our purpose, each Christian denomination defines its membership through a different mix of these three categories. For example, the Church of England often measures its participant membership through the numbers of those on the Electoral Roll (not to be confused with the local authority register of electors), yet this can include a number of people who are associate rather than participant members. The emphasis is heavily on Durkheim's category of affiliation. The Baptist Church measures those adults who are baptized as believers, putting the emphasis on Durkheim's third category of belief. And the Catholic Church measures the number of those baptized into the Catholic Church, which is neither a measure of (current) belief nor necessarily of practice, and not necessarily of affiliation either. Peter Brierley gives the fascinating example of the criterion for membership of the Nigerian New Life Church. It is simply an acceptable answer to the question: 'When did you last pray for a miracle?' At the same time, age differences come into play. Anglicans can be members of the Electoral Roll if they are 16 or over; Baptists can become full members if they are 14 or over. And so on. So the issue of membership numbers, even when these are available, is not straightforward.

What is useful is that these same figures are usually available over a specific period of time. While each denomination may collect its membership figures in a different way from other denominations, it usually uses the same criteria against time, and therefore the trends in membership of denominations can be usefully compared against each other. In the United Kingdom, it is clear that participant membership of the main Christian traditions has been steadily falling throughout the twentieth century, and that this decline has recently increased. In 1900 church membership was 33 per cent of the population; by 2000 it had dropped to 12 per cent (Brierley 2001: 56).

Another way of measuring participant membership is to count the number of people in church on any particular Sunday. This was first done on 30 March 1851 alongside the Census of Population of England and Wales and a census of educational provision (including Sunday Schools). That survey suggests that 39 per cent of the population was in church on that census day, but there is general agreement that the figures are less than entirely accurate (see, for example, Lawton 1978: 77–86). No attempt was made to filter out those who attended more than once on that day, and it is likely that smaller 'cottage meetings' of non-conformists were missed out. If the same percentage of double attendances had been counted then as were recorded in the count of 1903, then this figure would drop to 24 per cent. This count was designed to be one of active participants only. There had been considerable debate about including a question of religious belief in the accompanying population census; in the end, strong opposition in the House of Lords by the Bishops of Oxford and Salisbury, amongst others, prevented this. In the introduction to the 1854 report on the religious census, Horace Manns writes:

> it was considered that the outward conduct of persons furnishes a
> better guide to their religious state than can be gained by merely

vague professions. In proportion, it was thought, as people truely are connected with particular sects or churches, will be their activity in raising buildings in which to worship and their diligence in afterwards frequenting them; but where there is an absence of such practical regard for a religious creed, but little weight can be attached to any purely formal acquiescence. (Quoted in Moore 1988: 9§6.1.1.)

The *Daily News* undertook a large-scale study of church attendance in London between November 1902 and November 1903. This counted everyone going to every place of worship in a specific London borough for every service, counting a different borough every week. Excluding those who went more than once on the same day, the survey found that 19 per cent of the population of London attended church each Sunday. Again, this figure needs to be treated with caution and cannot necessarily be extrapolated to the rest of England, let alone the United Kingdom. We know from other research that the population of people attending church in rural areas can be considerably higher, so the overall figure of 19 per cent for London is possibly nearer the extrapolated 24 per cent estimate for the 1851 survey.

A Mass-Observation Survey in 1948–49 found that 15 per cent of the population attended church (Mass-Observation 1948). The English Church Census of 1979 found that 12 per cent of the population attended, and in 1989 the figure had dropped to 10 per cent. In 1998 the same method of counting showed a figure of $7\frac{1}{2}$ per cent.

What these figures appear to show is that the number of people attending church Sunday by Sunday has declined over the last 150 years, that decline becoming more rapid in the final two decades of the last century. But these are attendance figures, not membership figures. What the figures do not show, or at least what might be masked by the measurement, are those members who have changed their pattern of attendance from regular attendance Sunday by Sunday to less frequent attendance of, say, one in two or three Sundays. If the kind of pressures outlined in the last chapter have reduced the frequency of attendance rather than the number of people attending, then the impact of these attendance surveys on our perception of membership, rather than attendance, might not be so reliable. At the same time, there is a very large number of people attending only occasionally. A survey done by the Wakefield Diocese showed that 55 per cent of those attending churches in one particular deanery over a four-week period attended only once (Holmes 2001). These figures are, more or less, an indication of the participant membership of the Christian Church. By any measure they appear to show a relatively small percentage of the population, and one that is declining. But a very different picture begins to emerge if we broaden the criteria by which we measure the membership of the Christian churches. The British Social Attitudes Survey conducted in 1995 (National Centre for Social Research 1995) found that just under 33 per cent of the population said that they were Church of England, and a further 25 per cent said that they were members of another Trinitarian denomination. One in nine of those with a religious affiliation said that they attended services or meetings connected with their religion at least once a week. But around half said they never, or practically never, attended. The religious trends survey conducted in 1997 showed that two in three people (65 per cent) call themselves Christian, but only one in 11 actually attends on an average Sunday (National Centre for Social Research 1997).

A small survey that I commissioned from Gallup in 1996 as part of the preparation for the churches' celebration of the millennium was designed to find out the extent and source of the nation's knowledge of the Lord's Prayer. As part of that survey, Gallup asked their sample a simple question about religious affiliation. Fifty-four per cent claimed membership of the Church of England, and 22 per cent claimed membership of another Christian denomination. Only 19 per cent claimed that they had no religious denomination. These figures are significant in that they were not the main purpose of the survey, and in that they show as clearly as any other the gap between participant membership measured by the churches themselves, and associate membership claimed by individuals.

Research undertaken for the Diocese of Wakefield showed that in the Almondbury Deanery between 19 October and 7 December 2000, 55 per cent of church attenders were there only once (Holmes 2001). Blink and you miss them. But if this 55 per cent is at all representative of those who belong by association, attending only rarely, then there is a very large part of the Church that is not being nurtured or educated.

One of the most recent and significant surveys, undertaken by Gordon Heald of Opinion Research Business and coordinated by the Churches Information for Mission, was carried out between 7 and 9 December 2001 (Heald 2001). It was remarkably consistent with previous surveys that demonstrated the gap between participant and associate membership. Interviews were conducted by telephone with a nationally representative sample of 1,006 respondents, giving a sampling error of approximately plus or minus 3 per cent. The question 'Irrespective of whether you go to church, do you regard yourself as a Christian?' received the following answers:

4%   Refuse to answer or don't know
5%   I am a member of a non-Christian religion, so do not regard
     myself as a Christian
18% I do not regard myself as a Christian
73% Yes, I regard myself as a Christian

Given the context of the survey, the figure of 73 per cent for those who regard themselves as Christian would be remarkable were it not for its consistency with previous surveys that have shown similar, though slightly lower, numbers. Heald himself makes the point that the survey was done only a few weeks after the 11 September 2001 atrocities, suggesting that a 4 to 5 per cent inflation might be caused by people distancing themselves from Islam. He cites similar rises in American surveys. Even allowing for a 5 per cent 'distancing factor', the figure of 68 per cent remains a signficant fact for the churches. When the figures for those claiming a faith allegiance are broken down into their constituent parts, the results are even more illuminating:

1%   Jewish
1%   Muslim
1%   Hindu
3%   House churches
5%   Free Churches
5%   Church of Scotland
10% Catholic
52% Anglican

(Buddhists and Sikhs are too small a percentage of the population to measure accurately with a random sample of only one thousand respondents.)

Taking as a trend over time the remarkably large number of people who claim to belong to the Church of England, the number has risen from just under 33 per cent in 1995, through 44 per cent at Easter 2001, to 52 per cent at Christmas 2001. Whether the terrorist atrocities on 11 September and their aftermath have had an impact on associate membership is hard to say without further research. What can be said, however, with only minimal reservations, is that while participant membership of the Church of England is in slow decline, associate membership appears to be consistently large, if not actually growing.

The figures are put into a broader context when the full scope of the survey is taken into account. The purpose of the survey was to find out how the British planned to celebrate Christmas in 2001. The answers are illuminating (see Table 2.1)

Table 2.1: Survey of Christmas plans
Question: Which activities will you participate in this Christmas?

Activity	% respondents
Exchange presents	94
Have a special Christmas Day/Eve meal with your family	80
Decorate inside/outside your home	80
Have a turkey over the festive season	74
Buy Christmas crackers	66
Have an advent calendar	51
Listen to/view the Queen's speech	51
Buy a Christmas tree	49
Make a special donation to charity over Christmas	49
Attend a carol service	41
Make a Christmas cake/pudding	40
Attend nativity/Christmas service	35
Attend a religious service on Christmas Day/Eve	26
Visit a pantomime	25
Have a crib in your home	14
Pray at a crib in church	13
Spend it with friends but without your family	13
Work on Christmas Day	10
Have Christmas abroad	4
Spend Christmas alone	4
Do not celebrate Christmas	1

Over 40 per cent of the respondents to the survey planned to attend a carol service. About one third planned to attend a nativity or Christmas service, and a massive 25 per cent of the respondents planned to attend a religious service on Christmas Eve or Christmas Day. Having sat in Wells cathedral with my family for the midnight mass, I can confirm from personal experience that there was standing room only for that one service, and the church seats in the region of 1,500 people. By any account, these figures are impressive, and give the lie to those media reports that Christianity is dying. However, what they do not explain are the reasons for the gap between participant and associate membership. In any research, one of the indicators of significance is discontinuity. And there could hardly be a greater discontinuity than the 12–14 per cent membership claimed by the churches, and the 73 per cent (or so) claimed by individuals themselves.

It is at this point that the research fails us. Apart from a few broad surveys of social trends, or the passing measurement of claims for membership such as that described by Gallup, there is remarkably little research into the growing number of people who belong to the Church by association. Despite its many committees, with their vast expenditure on reports and position papers, the Church of England has no research group of its own on this subject, and can call on no organized network of academics who are already working in this field. Its mission appears to be guided solely by instinct, and in this case, as the CIM survey shows, its instincts may not be serving it well.

Membership 'Outside' the Church

There is a great deal of evidence that a majority of people, if not a large majority, have a sense of the transcendent that is quite independent of the Church. Jesus also appears to assume this direct relationship between his hearers and their God. He speaks directly to them, evoking not membership of the synagogue or temple, but a lifestyle of direct dependence on God, a life that is lived according to the claims of the Kingdom of God. Language that defines a faultline between people who are spiritual and those who are not is as alien to the New Covenant as it is to the Old. The assumption is that all of us, whether or not we are members of a worshipping community, are capable of recognizing and responding to the spiritual.

This approach is echoed in a different way by the zoologist Alister Hardy. He suggests that spiritual awareness is a biological phenomenon that has evolved through a process of natural selection because it has survival value. Whether or not evolutionary theory is the correct explanation for the phenomenon, it is increasingly recognized by most current researchers that somewhere in the region of 70 per cent of the population are willing to own some recognition of the spiritual. David Hay and Kate Hunt, in their paper 'Understanding the Spirituality of People Who Don't Go to Church', describe this undefined awareness:

> Another much larger group offered the commonest response of all, in that they were uneasy about saying anything positive about their spiritual experience, beyond the conviction that there is 'something there'; sometimes adding that it matters very much that it is there. This term 'something there' was so commonly used that we are thinking of drawing on it as the title of the book we are writing about the research. At one level this refusal to make positive statements suggests a widespread suspicion about the adequacy of traditional theological language to describe our experience of God. Perhaps

this is not surprising after 300 years of sustained critique of religions within European culture. (Hay and Hunt 2000: §5.6.1)

The age of reason was itself partly responsible for driving a wedge between what is 'rational' and what is 'spiritual', and the division led inexorably to the secular state. Yet almost daily in my parish visiting I would discover people who were quite deeply aware of the spiritual, while being quite certain that the Church, with all its demands, rituals and hierarchies, was not for them. I have already mentioned the council worker nearing retirement who put a decorated plaque in the front garden of his council house inscribed with the lines 'You are nearer to God in the garden than anywhere else on earth.' This seemed to me to be an act of witness quite divorced from church membership, but that nevertheless made a clear and unequivocal statement about the faith of its owner.

If the argument that spiritual awareness is an almost universal phenomenon is accepted, it does not mean that all such awareness is Christian, or even derived from a personal Christian history. I am not suggesting a kind of unrecognized universalism. But where individuals who are not regular, or even irregular, church members do claim to be Christian or members of a particular church, we need to take these claims seriously. For them, believing is belonging.

Nearly all the clergy and ministers that I speak with are aware that they have a 'fringe' membership. By this they mean the people who come occasionally, who perhaps take the church magazine, or who turn up at Christmas or Easter or Harvest Festival. But it is important to make a clear distinction between participant members who attend occasionally, and those who would claim allegiance but do not currently attend anywhere. Those who hold a theology based on salvation by correct doctrine, or even worse, salvation by church attendance, will find it difficult to envisage a community of people who hold an allegiance to Christian faith and belief but who are not members of any sacramental or worshipping community. Yet all the statistics show that they exist, and in considerable numbers. They are not 'fringe' members in the sense that they attend occasionally. These are people with a fairly clear Christian commitment, but who see no reason to be part of a worshipping community. For many of them, it will be mobility that has severed the link between faith and church membership. For others, it will be a sense that the worshipping community does not 'scratch where their faith itches'. Both John Finney and Professor Leslie Francis have done considerable research in this area, and their work is well worth reading (see, for example, Kay and Francis 1996: 141–58). But the key point to note here, and one that will be elaborated throughout the book, is that associate membership is not 'fringe' membership. It may become 'fringe' membership if the Church is able to engage with the issues and concerns of its associate members, but the two concepts are not the same. The essence of participation is involvement through physical presence. Participants are those who take part in something by being there themselves. Participant members of a church are those who worship regularly together, who form a physical community, who meet together regularly to worship, to celebrate the eucharist, to order and manage the business of the church. Their theology may differ markedly in many respects, but they are likely to share a common belief that the Church is a bit like Noah's Ark, saving them from drowning in the secular world. Membership of the Church of England, along with a number of other churches, is not necessarily dependent on Christian commitment or theological understanding. But our participants will be there, most Sundays, taking part in the life of the congregation. Their sense of belonging to God will be defined in terms of the theological culture of the congregation of which they are members, but it will be participant membership that distinguishes them from the world from which they have been saved.

The Failure of 'Participant' Thinking

The first problem with a theology of belonging that is primarily based on membership of the Church, and that does not point beyond itself to the community in which the Church is set, is that it is not a fully incarnational theology, and can even lead to the rejection of the most fundamental of all Christian doctrines, that of creation itself. It treats the world not as something created and celebrated by God, but as something to be saved from, and the Church as something to be saved into. It fosters a subtle kind of racism, where those who belong to the community of the Church are superior to those 'outside'. Even the language is questionable. It talks of membership in terms of belonging in a way that suggests the inferiority of those who belong to different communities, or none. It can lead to the loss of social engagement, and to the fragmentation of religious identity. It was, and remains, the first step on the road to the cult of Jesus that exists within so many of our churches. And when that membership is felt in terms not of faith in a living and forgiving God, but of adherence to a set of moral principles, it can lead to the worst kind of feelings of moral superiority over those amongst whom the Church is set.

The second problem is that this theology runs counter to an understanding of the relationship between God and his creation that permeates the Scriptures. What we see reflected there, particularly in the teaching of the three great prophets and in Jesus' own ministry, is something very different. It is an emphasis not on exclusion but on inclusion. God is not merely concerned with saving a remnant of us out of the wicked world into the safety of a faith community; he is concerned with the salvation, or healing, of the whole created order: 'It is too small a thing for you to be my servant to restore the tribes of Jacob and bring back those of Israel I have kept. I will also make you a light for the Gentiles, that you may bring my salvation to the ends of the earth' (Isaiah 49.6 RSV). While the nature of the operation may be imprecise, the scope is clear. God is not merely concerned with the Church; he is intimately concerned with the planet and all that is on it. The view of Scripture is that whoever we are, and whatever our religious belief or allegiance, we belong first to God; any other belonging is subordinate.

The third problem, and one that reflects our current concern more specifically, is that this narrow theology of belonging is distinctly at odds with our culture. We are increasingly a culture that demands direct access. We want direct access to education, to news, to sport, to banking, to insurance. We find the Internet appealing because it provides direct, individual access to information and communities of interest. And we instinctively feel that if there is a God, he should be a 'direct access' God. Put this alongside the rejection of received authority and the importance given to personal experience and personal spirituality, and it is little wonder that there is a gap between the rise in spiritual interest and the membership of churches and their attendance figures. And the problem for the Church is that the God of the new covenant colludes with this view; he really is a 'direct access' God!

But perhaps the most important reason why a theology of membership that restricts Christian discipleship to the Church's participant members is flawed is because it fails to recognize the most fundamental cultural change of all – that the Church is no longer the counter-culture to secularism because secularism itself is, if not dead, then certainly in terminal decline. In a postmodern culture, the absence of a meta-narrative does not simply mean that there is no overarching religious narrative; it further means that secularism is also rejected as the common, agreed meta-narrative. In fact, secularism, not faith, is the culture that is most at risk of rejection as an overarching world-view. In the sixties and seventies, it was not simply unfashionable to be a member of a faith community; it was old-fashioned, out of date and out of touch. But with the collapse of secularism, and the demise of socialism as a universal answer to our social ills, the death of God is no longer seen as an inevitable consequence of growing up. It is coming to be viewed more as the teenage rebellion of western society, which as it grows towards maturity is able not merely to be tolerant of different spiritualities, but to see them as essential to our survival and the survival of the planet.

The Church as a 'Waypoint' on our Spiritual Journey

In a culture where 88 per cent of the population rejects the suggestion that they are not 'a spiritual person' (Heald 1999), the Church no longer holds the monopoly of faith over against a secular society. We have been over-taken by a culture which is rapidly recognizing that individuals, and the communities they form, should celebrate and give time to values that go beyond the material. As a result of this sea-change in the values and beliefs of our culture, the institutional churches often appear more secular than the communities within which they are set. Spirituality is to be found outside, not inside, the Church.

For our postmodern culture, the Church is only useful in so far as it enhances the spiritual journey of the individual or small community. The analogy of the news media illustrates the point. Our culture is hungry for news, whether local, regional, national or international. In a global society, we need news in order to define our frame of reference, because without such a frame of reference we find it hard to make sense of our place in a global society. We can find that news on the television, in newspapers, on the radio, or on the Internet. We choose the medium most suited to us, but it is the news story itself, rather than the medium, that we relate to. Following the sudden tragic death of Princess Diana, millions of people followed the story through the print and broadcast media. Many of them shared a common experience of grief and shock, which brought to the surface unresolved grief from their own past. They sensed a kind of 'belonging' to each other in the grieving process. They may have sat in front of the television, or devoured the newspapers, or listened intently to the radio, but these media merely facilitated a relation-ship with the story, the myth of the modern princess, that drove them to visit London, to stand outside Kensington Palace, or to line the route of the funeral in their millions. The medium was only important insofar as it helped them engage with the unfolding story, the common experience of grief and the common ritual of mourning.

The spiritual relationship that God intends is not between the indi-vidual and the Church; it is between the individual and God himself. Jesus' own ministry makes this strikingly clear. In his parables, his teach-ing, even his death and resurrection, he deliberately stands outside the

Temple and the rabbinical structures. His message, as much by his actions as his words, is one of a direct relationship between the individual and the God of creation. And in an age of choice, individuals today are going to treat the Church in much the same way that they treat other agencies: as a potential resource to meet their own spiritual needs, as one choice among others, but not as an end in itself. The desire is for a direct and tangible spiritual relationship with God, however he is defined. The Church is useful only in so far as it is perceived to help with this quest.

Chapter 3

Belonging and Place

Belonging in Creation

For those who belong by association, whose believing itself forms the context of their sense of belonging to God, their relationship with place is important. After all, our spiritual journey does not begin with our entry into the Church, but with our place in the created order. We are not born into the Church, but into the world, as a new member of a community of creation that includes the trees and leaves of our surroundings, the rock and soil in which they grow, and the living things that populate them. All of these are God-given, an inheritance to be nurtured, celebrated, enjoyed and passed on in turn to our children as their inheritance.

Within our own culture, the growing awareness of ecology and the need to see our place as human beings in relationship with the planet, dependent upon it and responsible for its care, has led to a widespread rejection of any spirituality that does not have a high view of creation and our place within it. An awareness of the relationship between place, belonging and spirituality is therefore enormously important if we are to value and nurture those who belong by association. Each of us is born into a specific place, and we are dependent upon it to support us and nurture us as we grow. Just as the infant develops a bond with its parents, so the growing child develops a bond with its surroundings. We gain stability through our relationship with the earth, the land, the geography of our home, and it is as important to our spiritual awareness as the relationship we have with our mothers and fathers.

Belonging and Leaving

Belonging is fundamental to human life and health. At the moment of birth we are embraced by the warmth of our mother, and as we grow so our circle of belonging grows and expands with us. At first, the infant's sense of its identity is indistinct from its sense of its mother, and the mother's absence in itself creates distress because it causes a confusion of

27

identity. But slowly the infant begins to gain an awareness of itself as distinct from its mother. The need for closeness is still there, but there can be substitutes. The teddy bear becomes a substitute for mum's presence, a transitional substitute. Other family members gain attention, and slowly the child builds up a sense of belonging to a community, and therefore of being an individual in its own right in a small community of other individuals where he or she is loved and valued and nurtured for him- or herself.

Growing up becomes a process of excursions from the safety of the parent into the world around. A child will repeatedly return to the security of 'mum' or 'dad' as a support for his or her exploration, and the sense of security created by mum or dad 'simply being there' enables the child to take the many small risks involved in maturing into a healthy adult. As the process continues, the child achieves the self-confidence to leave mum and dad, and to become an individual. The teenage years are marked by this transitional process, and can be as threatening to the parents as they are to the child. But a really healthy adult is aware of both the need to belong and the need to be free.

Of course, a lot can go wrong and sadly it sometimes does. Children can become isolated and distant from their parents; parents can become overprotective because they themselves were unable to grow into being fully independent themselves. The tension between self-confidence and the need to belong can create all sorts of problems.

As the child grows, it also differentiates between its own identity and the identity of its environment. At first, its environment is perceived as an extension of itself. But slowly the child comes to recognize, and then value, its environment as part of the nurturing of its own identity. Place becomes as important as person, and the surroundings that the child begins to explore become a second mother to it. Little wonder, then, that the bonds of attachment to place can be very strong indeed.

In a similar way, our spiritual development needs both the support of a mature spiritual community, and the independence to grow its own identity. A church that sees 'belonging' simply in terms of presence or regular attendance, that tries to control or dictate belief and practice, and that interprets any sign of spiritual independence as loss of faith or commitment, may damage the spiritual development of the individual concerned and promote the one thing it most fears – the loss of the individual as he or she rejects the overbearing control or restrictive boundaries. In the same way, too much freedom can give the impression that faith makes no claims, that there are no challenges, and that it really doesn't matter what you believe. Just as growing children need the freedom to explore, as well as the security of elastic but firm boundaries, so too as individuals we need both freedom and security in order to explore and develop our spiritual identities.

And so our sense of belonging is, to a large extent, conditioned by our relationships and our sense of identity with the place or places we know. We are creatures of place, and belong together within specific locations that we call 'home'. The word 'displacement' is itself revealing; to be a 'displaced person' is not only to lose one's home, but to be at risk of losing one's sense of belonging, even one's sense of identity. It is no accident that one of the key features of the new paganism is an emphasis on the spirit of 'place'. 'Knowing your place' is an uncomfortable phrase indicating a restriction of movement, a place where you belong and movement from which means that you are trespassing on someone else's belonging. And salvation, in both the old and new covenant, is sometimes described in terms of liberation from an inappropriate restriction of place.

One of the dominant features of our culture is its high degree of mobility. For many of us, this mobility means that our sense of belonging to a specific place has been diminished, even extinguished. This is not the pilgrimage experience of our spiritual ancestors, whose identity was forged by a place that they had not yet reached. Rather it is a genuine alienation, a disconnectedness that pervades our families and our working lives. Our search for meaning, for values, for transcendence is linked with our often unconscious longing for a physical location that we know, and where we are known. Our recognition of the transcendent is at least in part dependent on our recognition of the sacredness of place.

As the book of Genesis opens, we see the Spirit of God hovering over the unformed chaos of matter. The story, of course, is mythical, poetic, and the truth it contains is all the stronger for that. But the language has the same overtones of sexuality as in the story of the Annunciation. Compare the two:

> In the beginning, when God created the universe, the earth was formless and desolate. The raging ocean that covered everything was engulfed in total darkness, and the Spirit of God was moving over the water. (Genesis 1:1–2 GNB)

> And the angel answered and said unto her, The Holy Ghost shall come upon thee, and the power of the Highest shall overshadow thee: therefore also that holy thing which shall be born of thee shall be called the Son of God. (Luke 1.35 AV)

In both cases, the sense of the passage is one of the impregnation of matter by the Spirit of God. In Genesis, the Hebrew verb *m'rahepet*, translated variously as 'moving over' (RSV and others), 'moved upon' (AV), or 'hovering over' (New Living Translation), is a strong, active verb[1]. Its meaning is not quite the same as the Greek verb *episkiadzo*, used by Luke in his annunciation passage, which is usually interpreted fairly literally as 'overshadowing', and which has a slightly more passive sense than the strong, almost violent *m'rahepet*. Yet the meanings are clearly similar. In both cases, the verb is an analogy for making pregnant. In Genesis, the Spirit of God makes matter pregnant with both purpose and spirit. In Luke, the Spirit of God makes Mary pregnant with the Christ child. As so often happens, the Old Testament foreshadows the New. There are critical differences, to be sure, between the creation of matter, which is 'made' (the narrative goes on to make that clear in a series of statements, each of them beginning 'And God said . . . and there was') and the incarnation of Jesus, who is said in the creeds to be 'begotten, not made', and 'of the same substance as the Father'. But there are too many similarities in the analogies for us to ignore this aspect of the creation narrative.

This understanding of creation as the first great expression, or incarnation, of God may well be a high view of creation, and it may well stretch the traditional Christian distinction between matter and spirit, but it is inherent in the Scriptures, and is fundamental to a Christian understanding of nature. This stuff of which we are made, which we share with our brother and sister creatures, is not a merely accidental genetic development. This 'stuff', or whatever name you give to the living rock, stone, tree, leaf and teeming life of which we are a part, is sacred. The world of plants, animals, buzzing insects and active volcanoes is the first great incarnation. It is shot through with the life, the essence, of God. Formless matter has indeed been made pregnant by the Spirit of God, and it has given birth to a wonderful, rich and sacred variety of living things – even St Paul, writing within the Greek tradition of the separation of spirit and matter, reaches out to grasp the import of the underlying Hebrew analogy:

> Ever since God created the world, his invisible qualities, both his eternal power and his divine nature, have been clearly seen; they are understood through the things that God has made. (Romans 1.20 RSV)

So it should come as no surprise to our own materialist generation that those who claim faith in God, or allegiance to the Christian church, without ever expressing membership of any particular denomination or congregation, very often reflect a similar theology of creation to those who stand right outside the Christian tradition. We understand nature as 'sacred'. We recognize the awesome power and beauty of God in the things he has made, and we naturally, even unconsciously, seek to express solidarity with his creation. In this sense, faith is as natural to humans as leaves are to trees. Arguments about doctrine are, in this sense, irrelevant, because doctrine is merely the precipitation of understanding, or the development of a framework of words, that allows us to communicate our understanding of God within the context of faith.

This brings sharply into focus the issue of the relationship between us as human beings and the creation of which we are a part. And here, the language of Genesis (or at least, the Authorized Version) is at first sight decidedly unhelpful:

And God said, Let us make man in our image, after our likeness: and let them have dominion over the fish of the sea, and over the fowl of the air, and over the cattle, and over all the earth, and over every creeping thing that creepeth upon the earth. (Genesis 1.26 AV)

The misunderstanding of those two little words 'dominion over' has caused untold suffering for millions of people worldwide, not to mention our brother and sister animals, and the plants and other living things that share the same earth, air, fire and water as we do. That misunderstanding has pandered to human arrogance, and justified human greed.

But used in this way those words are a poor expression both of the theology of divine 'dominion' and of the intention of the writer. A much better expression in today's culture of domination would be that of the 'care-taker'. Women and men are to be care-takers – to look after our fellow-creatures, and to seek their well-being and the well-being of the universe that sustains them. Read in this context, the whole purpose of humanity is re-defined:

And God said, Let us make man in our image, after our likeness: and let them be care-takers of the fish of the sea, and of the fowl of the air, and of the cattle, and of all the earth, and of every creeping thing that creepeth upon the earth.

So far, we have spoken in a general way about a Christian understanding of the spiritual nature of creation, and the relationship between human beings and the world within which we live. The landscape is shot through with the divine nature, and our task is to recognize the value of both earth and spirit, and, to put it simply, to celebrate the presence of the Spirit of God in the natural world he has created and which he inhabits.

But we need to move from the general to the specific – to the sacredness of place. And here it seems to me that in the Christian tradition, place is sacred in two ways.

First, it is sacred wherever we place the fences because it is always a specific example of the universal sacredness of creation. Put another way, because all of creation is sacred, so is this specific place, this specific tree or animal or sea or village. And because each place is a specific example of a universal reality, each specific place is a symbol for the sacredness of the whole. Thus an offence against the sacredness of the specific is an offence against the whole.

I remember vividly a picture taken at the end of the First World War of a wood somewhere in France, scarred and broken by shellfire. There was something about the damage caused by the shelling that was an offence not only against humanity, but against the place itself. On a much smaller scale Network Rail, the post-privatization company currently responsible for the British rail network, have to trim the branches of the trees growing near the tracks to limit the amount of leaves on the line. But instead of respecting the integrity of the trees, they use a flail to rip and shred the branches. This results in long stretches of shattered branches with bark ripped off or shredded, with no care whatsoever shown to the integrity of their growth. The trees and shrubs are treated as mere 'things' to be beaten back, made uglified and broken, simply because Network Rail find it cheaper to use flails than to use people. This is not just a matter of appearance. It is a matter of respect for the spirituality of creation.

Second, place becomes sacred because some places are specific to a meeting with God in special ways. Meeting with God is usually place-specific because we humans are place-specific. We meet with God in our garden, or our favourite grove, or our church or chapel. For me, the garden tomb in Jerusalem and the River Thames at Streatley are both sacred places for that reason. So is the chapel at my monastic college, and for much the same reason. It is in those specific places that I have had a particularly vivid or rich encounter with God. Many of us can point to specific instances where God, or at least a sense of the sacred, has been encountered. And by definition, such instances are place-specific. We recognize them, and create a special place for them in our spiritual landscape. There are plenty of biblical references to places that have become sacred because of individual encounters with God. Moses' encounter with God at the burning bush is one of the best-known examples:

> Then he said, 'Do not come near; put off your shoes from your feet, for the place on which you are standing is holy ground.' And he said, 'I am the God of your father, the God of Abraham, the God of Isaac,

and the God of Jacob.' And Moses hid his face, for he was afraid to look at God. (Exodus 3.5–6 RSV)

And where this meeting with God is communal rather than individual, the concept of sacred place is both widened and strengthened.

A third way in which place becomes sacred is through its repeated use for worship over a period of time. Monastic gardens are a good example. So are a large number of churches and many sacred sites. Infusion with the divine spirit, or the thinning of the veil between spirit and creation, is another way of putting it. Some people talk about the stones of a building being drenched with the prayers of the saints. These places are sacred because worship has happened continually in these specific places over a period of time. This is the recognition of a spiritual reality – that this place or that place really is indwelt with the Divine in a special way because of the centuries of worship that have taken place here.

And of course, the reverse is true. You can find places where spiritual darkness, rather than light, is the operative force. Such places are uncomfortable, depressing (sometimes even contributing to clinical depression). I worked in such a place for nine years, and I suspect that such places are only healed through prayer and fasting.

And then, of course, nature itself sanctifies, or brings a sense of the sacred into our presence. At a very local level, the pot-plant in the midst of the barren office is a good example – or the tree in the car park; the wild wood under threat from developers; the forest under threat from loggers. All of these speak of the Divine in the midst of human activity. They become the spirit-bearers, the specific that points to the universal. You only have to visit a run-down urban housing estate to recognize the spiritual importance of nature – and the sanctifying effect of the creation of a small park or garden. It quite literally brings God into the place where he has been driven out. We do not worship the plants or the trees, but we do recognize in them the same spiritual origin as the rest of creation; they are sacred in the same sense that the planet is sacred – it is born of spirit overshadowing matter, and in its sacred beauty it brings us into the presence of God himself.

Conditioned as we are to thinking of our faith primarily in terms of salvation theology, or the theology of the cross and the resurrection, this sense of nature as being a 'God-bearer' may strike us as a pagan concept. But it is far from pagan, or at least, it is one of the points of commonality between Christianity and paganism. One of the greatest hymns, 'How Great Thou Art', begins:

O Lord my God, when I in awesome wonder
Consider all the works thy hand hath made,
I see the stars, I hear the mighty thunder,
Thy power throughout the universe displayed.

St Paul, in the letter to the Romans, draws from the might and majesty of
nature an argument not only for the existence of God, but for a reflection
of his nature in creation itself: 'Ever since the creation of the world, his
invisible nature, namely, his eternal power and deity, has been clearly
perceived in the things that have been made' (Romans 1.20 RSV). The
recognition of deity within the natural order is not something invented
by St Paul, nor is it confined to the new covenant. Genesis itself understands the creation in terms of an impregnation of chaos with spirit,
bringing into being the fecundity and creativity of nature and ultimately
of humankind. Jesus himself, in choosing the words 'Son of Man' as a self-
description in preference to 'Son of God', offers us a picture that resonates
with this sense of the immanence of God in nature. As James Jones,
Bishop of Liverpool, has said (in personal communication), the Hebrew
phrase *ben 'adam*, son of man, can be translated quite literally as 'son of
the one hewn from the earth'.

And if, standing on a mountain and seeing the majesty and awe of the
creator reflected in creation, you get a sense of the majesty of God, it is not
too big a step to take to see the whole reflected in the particular. A small
stone reminds us of the mountain. A plant reminds us of the wildness of
nature. It is no accident that the greatest saints see the face of Christ reflected in the greatest sinners. Some Christian scientists argue that their
spirituality has been formed not by reading the Bible, but by reading the
periodic tables – by seeing in the intricacies of nature the hand of the
Divine. Like Jacob's vision of the ladder between heaven and earth, our
own response on recognizing God in the things that he has made is quite
naturally to revere them as sacred: 'Surely, the Lord is in this place, and I
did not know it' (Genesis 28.16 NASB). Thus a specific place can become
for any of us a special place, a place where, like Jacob, we have met with the
Divine. It is sacred not simply because of our own subjective experience in
that it holds special meaning for us, even though it might, but because of
an objective reality. It reflects within itself the sacredness of the whole; it
reveals to us something about the nature of God himself. Of course, a lot
of the language we use to describe this sense of the sacredness of nature is
poetic, but that is one of the problems of religious language. We use words
of limited meaning to describe what is for each of us a special and sacred
mystery. The Christian can say with all the force of Scripture that this

plant, this mountain, this creature is sacred, not simply because it has been made by God, but because it has been conceived by the Spirit and shares the nature of God himself. This is the first great lesson of the Bible; that God became incarnate through the overshadowing of chaos by his Spirit, making it pregnant with meaning and purpose.

Our sense of place, and our understanding of it as sacred, is an essential part of a Christian sense of belonging. Our first allegiance is not to our local church, but to the God who has created us and given us a specific place to care for and to nurture at a specific time. In a fallen world, we will need the support, the teaching and the encouragement – in short, the resources – of the Church to nurture us in this task, but as growing and maturing Christians, we also need the freedom to develop a sense of identity that is separate and distinct from the Church so that we can take our proper place as caretakers of his creation, rather than mere participants in a religious organization. Membership of a particular congregation is not a prerequisite for this sense of belonging. But identification with place, and particularly with our own sacred places, probably is.

Within the context of the Old Testament, God reveals himself first to a people defined by place. To the people of Israel he says: 'You will be my people, and I will be your God' (Ezekiel 36.28 NRSV). The God of the Old Testament is a desert God, a God of sand and heat, a God of harsh places and difficult terrain. The symbols and imagery used to describe the experience of God in the Old Testament are those of the desert and the mountains, of a place that is as familiar to its inhabitants as it is alien to us. Our understanding of God is place-specific, because it uses the imagery of place as the context and language of discovery. It is the same in the New Testament. Trying to explain the imagery of shepherds and lambs to an urban junior school demonstrates this only too clearly.

The linkage between belonging to a spiritual community and belonging to a particular place is probably as ancient as humanity. The earliest records reveal the deep human need to link particular gods to particular places, and visitors to those places would make offerings to the gods of the places they visited. There is some evidence that they would also take their own family, or familiar, gods with them when they travelled, creating a kind of capsule of 'place' that travelled with them. An example of these household gods is found in the story of Laban in Genesis 31: 'Laban had gone to shear his sheep, and during his absence Rachel stole the household gods that belonged to her father' (Genesis 36.19 GNB). These gods were significant in providing protection for the family, and would have been taken with the family as it moved from place to place. They provided a clear link between place – whatever place at which the family was camped – and their sense of relationship with the gods who protected them.

But perhaps even more significant is the desire to return to the family 'home' for burial. On the death of Sarah his wife, Abraham buys a cave and the surrounding land as a resting place. The account is quite specific in stressing Abraham's need for ownership. Abraham approaches the resident community, the Hittites, saying: 'I am a foreigner living here among you; sell me some land, so that I can bury my wife.' The Hittites offer to give him what he needs: 'Listen to us, sir. We look upon you as a mighty leader; bury your wife in the best grave that we have. Any of us would be glad to give you a grave so that you can bury her.' But Abraham insists on buying it, getting into what seems quite an argument with the owner, Ephron. The point Abraham makes is clear: 'Ask him to sell it to me for its full price, here in your presence, so that I can own it as a burial-ground' (Genesis 23 GNB). This sense of ownership of place is enormously important to Abraham, even though the cost, only four hundred pieces of silver, is described as minimal. The place has to belong to him and his family in perpetuity, and he and his family belong to that place. It becomes a rooted place, somewhere that the family will look upon for generations to come as their place.

Later, we read of the death and burial of Jacob. His instructions to his sons are quite specific: 'Now that I am going to join my people in death, bury me with my fathers in the cave that is in the field of Ephron the Hittite, at Machpelah, east of Mamre, in the land of Canaan. Abraham bought this cave and field from Ephron for a burial ground. That is where they buried Abraham and his wife Sarah; that is where they buried Isaac and his wife Rebecca: and that is where I buried Leah. The field and the cave in it were bought from the Hittites. Bury me there' (Genesis 49.29–32 GNB).

Again, when we read of the death of Joseph in Egypt, a similar request is made: 'He said to his brothers, "I am about to die, but God will certainly take care of you and lead you out of this land to the land he solemnly promised to Abraham, Isaac, and Jacob. Promise me", he said, "that when God leads you to that land, you will take my body with you."' (Genesis 50.24–5 RSV).

The sense of a place being sacred to a family is not confined to the people of the old covenant; it is alive and well today. It was not long after I had taken on my first incumbency that I discovered that a family of travellers regarded the parish church as their sacred place. One of their children died, and the undertaker quite specifically insisted that despite the fact that they travelled across the United Kingdom, and that their current winter quarters were a considerable distance from my parish, they nevertheless regarded this place as 'home' because it had been a place of belonging for many generations. They apparently returned to this church and this place for their significant weddings and funerals, and my job, as present guardian of their spiritual home, was to take this funeral. I travelled out to their current encampment to visit them, and was struck by the sense they had of the church being 'theirs'. I duly took the funeral, and large numbers of trucks arrived loaded with flowers and wreaths spelling out the name of the child, or various exhortations. There were far too many people to enter the church – the men mostly congregated outside – and I estimated that at the graveside there must have been a crowd of at least a thousand people. This was the first of a number of rites of passage that I conducted for various branches of that particular travelling family. The importance to them was not the person who took the particular service, but the place itself.

We see much the same association between family and place at weddings and baptisms. Young people who have grown up and moved away very often return to 'their' parish church to be married, or to have their children baptized. If asked, they will often say that it is where their parents lived, or where they grew up. Their sense of the sacred place is strong, and is often clearly linked with their parents or grandparents. This may be as a result of the ministry of a particular person – ordained or lay – in their early years, or it may be the result of earlier residence. But there is a clearly defined and common pattern of belonging to a specific sacred place that is both strong in its emotional pull, and clearly identifiable with a specific building. It is interesting to look at the theology that lies behind the choice. Very often, if probed, there is a sense of recognition that while God is present in most churches (maybe not all – modern buildings are often suspect), this particular church is identified with God's dealings with the family in the past, and that it is to this place, where God is specific to that particular family, that they wish to return. The individuals concerned may not attend church regularly. If they did, they would very soon invest their new church with greater significance, or at least they would find that their worship would invest them with a greater sense of local belonging. But as we have seen, membership by participation is not the only form of membership, and these couples have a sense of belonging that is driven not by attendance but by past experience. They form a recognizable part of the congregation of that particular place, even though they may be completely unknown to the current incumbent or the current participant congregation. For them, believing and belonging go together, but both are rooted in a place that may be many hundreds of miles and many years distant.

It is very important that we recognize their membership, and celebrate it rather than reject it when they turn up, often 'out of the blue', for specific rites of passage. These people form a clear part of the church's membership by association. If asked, they would very probably declare a membership of the Church, and if pressed, would identify with a particular church building that may be a considerable distance from their current residence. We live in such a fragmented society that these tenuous ties to the past are easily damaged, but they form an important part of the network of relationships that we need to celebrate in order to minister effectively to the needs of these people. Yet all too often we hear accounts of these links being devalued. The process of special licences for marriage rites recognizes people's need to return to a particular family 'sacred place', but the difficulty and cost of obtaining such licences, and the relatively recent emphasis on the rite happening in the current parish of residence, devalues their sense of membership and cuts right across the Church's mission. It has displaced a large number of these links.

The matter is made considerably worse by the current insistence by the Church of England on residence qualifications for marriage where one or more partners has been divorced. The recognition of failure, and the need to make a new beginning – to do it 'properly' this time around – very often drives this kind of associate member back to his or her sacred place, only to discover the door firmly closed. The experience of rejection can cause immense damage to the mission of the Church. The cumulative effect of an insistence on membership by participation in these cases is enormous. There is a large and growing percentage of the population that has been turned away from their 'sacred place' by such insistence, and that has experienced it as rejection. Marriage services in churches are declining at a frightening rate, while marriages in secular places licensed for such services is growing rapidly.

The 1994 Marriage Act enabled civil marriages to be solemnized on premises approved for the purpose by local authorities. But it specifically forbids those marriages to have any religious content: 'No religious service shall be used at a marriage on approved premises in pursuance of section 26(1)(bb) of this Act.' This means that anyone wishing to have a Christian marriage in a secular place approved by the local authority is unable to do so. Because of the 1994 Marriage Act, many couples are choosing to get married in places other than their parish church or the local register office. The range of such places has rapidly expanded, and as a result, the numbers of couples taking advantage of the new law has greatly increased. In 1995, the first year that the Act was in force, 2,496 couples were married in licensed premises. In 1999, that figure had leapt to 37,709[2]. From April 1995, when weddings in 'approved premises' were first permitted, ceremonies quadrupled in proportional terms from 1 in 71 marriages in 1995/6 to 1 in 18 of all marriages in 1996/7[3]. In a similar period, Church of England wedding services fell from 79,616 (1995) to 63,371 (1998), a drop of 16,245. This fall in the number of church weddings more or less mirrors the drop in the total number of wedding services nationally, from 268,344 in 1995 to 249,490 in 1999[4]. If this trend continues at roughly the same speed, by as early as 2004 the number of weddings in approved premises could outnumber those taking place in church.

The result of the ban on religious services at licensed premises has not only had a serious impact on the numbers of Christian marriages in recent years, and consequently on the amount of teaching that the Church has been able to give on the values of Christian family life, but will continue to have an increasingly detrimental effect on the ability of the Church to teach Christian family values in the future. Even if a couple are not regular participants in church worship, the time they spend with a Christian minister in preparing for their wedding can be used for highly valuable teaching, as well as establishing a relationship with the Church that can last the rest of their lives and provide a source of support and help should they meet family difficulties in the future.

Yet there is nothing in the teaching of Jesus, or of the Old or New Testament, that requires membership of a particular congregation as a precondition of grace. Nowhere is the spirituality of the people of God dependent on membership of a specific religious community. Under the old covenant, God deals not with a congregation but with a population. He is recognized as lawgiver, as the one who delivers from oppression 'with a mighty hand and an outstretched arm', but this deliverance is not conditional on membership of a local congregation. In the new covenant, God deals with a population, not a congregation. Jesus teaches those who are prepared to listen. He teaches in the marketplace, on the hillside, in the streets and in the countryside. His call is to whomever is willing to hear him, regardless of their village of origin. Neither is the experience of the transcendent limited to members of the Temple community, nor later to the worshippers at the synagogue. The Temple is there to provide a focus for worship, but not as the only means to worship. The relationship of the old covenant is between the population, the people of Israel, and God himself. That it came to be seen as a relationship in need of mediation through the Levitical priesthood is a development of the concept of atonement, rather than a necessary prerequisite for faith. The underlying theme of the old covenant is the direct relationship between God and his people.

Jesus also appears to assume this direct relationship between his hearers and their God. He speaks directly to them, evoking not membership of the synagogue or Temple, but a lifestyle of direct dependence on God, a life that is lived according to the claims of the Kingdom of God. Language that defines a faultline between people who are spiritual and those who are not is as alien to the new covenant as it is to the old. The assumption is that all of us, whether or not we are members of a worshipping community, are capable of recognizing and responding to the spiritual – that all of us can recognize the sacred, and that many will respond to it with awe and commitment, regardless of previous membership of any kind of congregation or religious community.

If this is so, then our understanding of the importance of place in our relationship with God is a function not of salvation, but of creation. We are creatures, born into an environment that helps to shape us and our attitudes to each other. It has long been said that Protestantism is a religion of cold climates, while Catholicism is a religion of hot climates. If there is any truth in this, and there may well be, it is because of the effect of our environment on our temperament, and therefore on our spirituality. The place where we are born, where we grow up, and with which we form a strong bond, is bound to affect our spirituality and our sense of relationship with God. This function of creation should not be lightly dismissed. It helps to create our self-identity and therefore shapes our sense of the sacred. We feel that we 'belong' within a particular culture, that we fit into a particular landscape, because we have grown with it; it has helped to shape us and make us what we are. The sense of dislocation when someone from 'up north' moves down south is very strong indeed. Equally, families can suffer a considerable identity crisis when they move from the south to the north of England. If this is true within one nation, it is certainly true cross-culturally. Moving from one part of the world to another can be a hugely disorientating experience, something that mission agencies have recognized and built into their training. Moving back can be even more disorientating, as we experience a change of values and financial environment. When we have been working in an environment where scraping together enough money for a meal is the norm for the majority of the population, moving back to an affluent western culture can be a distressing experience.

Like Laban with his household gods, we too take our spiritual environment with us like a small capsule. Our believing provides us with a sense of belonging that is both comfort and normality. When we move, we look for an environment that mirrors, more or less, the spiritual landscape we have left. This is why we find full-blown Victorian Anglicanism in the middle of Africa. This is why the search in a new place for a church that will suit us is so often a barren exercise. We become alienated, and look back to the place we have left as the place of our 'belonging'. Our believing becomes our belonging, and provides both the shape and the context for our faith. The real task in such circumstances is to embrace the sense of alienation and disorientation so that our faith can take on the new landscape in which we find ourselves. It is only when we are able to let go of the place of our ancestors that we can experience the liberation of the gospel. It was the same for Abraham, called to leave the place of his forebears, and to travel with his new relationship with God into unexplored territory.

The importance of transition has not really been recognized by the Church. We assume that if one of our participant members moves, they can and will make contact with a local church in their new area, and we wish them farewell. It has been demonstrated almost beyond doubt that one of the biggest causes of drift from the mainstream denominations is the mobility of our western population, with its consequent fracturing of relationships, but we do little to reduce the problem. Clearly, one of the most important things that any congregation can do is to maintain contact and relationship with those of its members who have moved away. To retain their membership, possibly for a number of years, can be a very helpful transitional process, and pastoral care of these 'past members' can be very valuable in helping them establish new patterns of believing and belonging in their new home. The development of e-mail lists, and the occasional telephone call and invitation to support some activity or other that is taking place in the 'old' church, can be extremely helpful in creating a climate of transition that maintains the family or individual member in participant membership.

On the other hand, for those who belong by association, the loss of identity through geographical movement is likely to be less acute, but more easily damaged when they attempt to return to their 'sacred place' and experience what they feel as rejection in some form or other. Like Jacob, they may wish to return to their rooted place when they die. Reservation of grave space in a familiar graveyard is evidence of this. But they are much more likely to wish to return for other rites of passage: for marriage or the baptism of children. These requests, far from being inappropriate, are signs of membership that the local church should take very seriously indeed. By creating a welcoming environment, and particularly by maintaining contact after the event, the local church can extend its ministry considerably, and can very often help to enable a transition to a new sacred place as well as effect some useful education and formation on the way.

But what happens when we move from one spiritual landscape to another? If believing really is the truest form of belonging, then our belief structures will give us at least as much security as our environmental structures. As we saw earlier, change in our spiritual landscape is an essential part of spiritual growth. But the move from one landscape to another, or even the gradual widening of our horizons, can become as alienating as a move from one country to another. We no longer seem to 'fit' into the old cultures in which we learned our faith. We have become strangers in the pilgrimage, moving into new spiritual territory. Again, the support we receive from those whom we have left behind will be crucial in helping us to make new links with those with whom we wish to explore new directions. This is not a matter of losing one's faith, although it can feel like that at the time; it is rather a matter of developing new ways of believing, taking with us all that we have learned from the past and using it to navigate a new course for the future. We may well develop the need to return from time to time to the place that gave us spiritual birth. Like Jacob, we may wish to return there when we die. But the pilgrimage is ours, and does not belong to anyone else. The task of the Church is to welcome and celebrate those who pass through, recognizing that they too are pilgrims for whom our hospitality and welcome is an essential part of their pilgrimage.

For many of our churches, this requires both a change of mind and a change of heart. It requires us to alter our conceptual geography so that our building and community are no longer 'our church', but 'their church'. And it requires us to recognize that while a particular individual or family might appear 'out of the blue' for a particular rite of passage, within their spiritual landscape our church is 'their' church and has been so for a long time. It may well be the focus of relationship between that family and God himself. Such a recognition requires us to change our attitudes to our associate members. It requires us to adopt a frame of mind that is open to all who seek to engage with the sacredness of things, where we welcome all who wish to travel with us for however long (or short) their journey. There should be no barriers to participation, but rather a celebration of homecoming for those whose believing has formed around a particular place, no matter how long ago, or how tenuous the physical linkage.

All this is, of course, dependent on the fact that people have a spiritual 'home'. In our fragmented society, this may well not be the case. There are many people who, sensing the lack of a spiritually rooted place of their own, begin the search. It will probably be at critical moments of their life – at marriage, at the birth of their first child, at a moment of physical crisis – that they hunt around for spiritual support, and feel the need for this rootedness. Their search may lead them outside the neat, parochial boundaries of the Church of England, or the congregational patterns of other denominations. The current fashion for commercial 'wedding fairs' can often create precisely these kinds of 'problems' for institutional churches. But the proper response from any of the churches is one of acceptance, guidance and welcome. Our task is to help them to form such relationships, to identify with a sacred place, and in the process to become more whole.

Chapter 4

Ark or Signpost?

When I was ten years old, living in rural Berkshire, I decided one Sunday morning to cycle the mile or so to the local parish church to attend the Sunday service. It was, on reflection, probably one of the first 'adult' decisions I had taken. Neither of my parents were regular churchgoers. But I had recently joined the church school in the local village after a highly unsatisfactory year at a private school in nearby Reading, and I had experienced even at a distance a new kind of community – a spiritual community. Met at the church door by Bill that morning, I was handed a small black Book of Common Prayer and a dark blue copy of *Hymns Ancient and Modern*. Shown to a box pew where the doors were held shut by little rotating brass clips, I sat through 11.00 a.m. sung matins. Even in 1960 it was another world, an alien world, where one learned to stand up and sit down at the right moment, and listened to a retired major stumbling through the difficulties of King James English. The village choir, dressed in Victorian costumes and sporting a full colonel (who did much for mission by giving each of the choir children a box of humbugs at Christmas), sang an anthem while the sunlight painted the dust with the colours of the stained glass. Over thirty years later, invited back to preach, I was met at the same church door by the same Bill, and handed the same prayer book for the same 11.00 a.m. service of matins. Unspoiled by progress, the Alternative Service Book, or radical theology, this stately ship of faith was still holding its course.

The analogy of the ship is not mine; it was the underlying narrative of that particular congregation, and has been that of many congregations across the denominations since the time of the great councils of the Church. One children's talk I remember vividly was based on this theology of belonging. The vicar asked us to look up at the shape of the roof. It was like a ship upside-down, he said. Like an ark. Like a new version of Noah's Ark, saving us from the flood of sin and judgement. Joining the Church was as necessary for salvation as passage on the ark was for the avoidance of drowning.

This, too, is the theology that colours the thinking of many of our participant members. They come to join the ship of faith, perhaps initially because they hope to find a sense of belonging that is missing elsewhere in their lives, or perhaps because they feel the need of a supportive spiritual community. They may come simply because they wish to explore the Christian faith, but this is less often the case. More often, initial involvement is through the many activities of the local parish: the toddlers' groups, lunch clubs, youth groups, coffee mornings – in fact, the host of small groups that engage with community need in its various forms.

This is, of course, a classic theology of mission – that of the 'fishing net' – where the Church, permeating the whole of the local community, provides a 'way in' for those who are seeking, or perhaps accidentally discovering, that membership by participation gives them a deeper and richer sense of belonging to God, and helps them to feel much more a part of the community to which they aspire, from which they feel in some degree alienated. But the model must not stop there. The Church itself, the community of participant members, is a community of support and nourishment for those who do not come – both those who belong by association and those who have yet to discover any sense of belonging with God.

It is not surprising that most churches today operate their mission on the basis of participative membership. Part of the problem is the heavy emphasis placed in previous generations on the covenant relationship. But if we are to be set free to explore new ways of belonging, we need to look again at our traditional understanding of covenant relationships, the important role they played in forming the sense of belonging under the old covenant, and the way that our focus of belonging has changed under the new covenant. In particular, we need to see how the symbols of those relationships, particularly baptism and eucharist, have been interpreted both by the Church and by popular culture, and the relationship of both to the belief and sense of belonging of participant and associate members.

The emphasis in the old covenant on the role of the extended family, or tribe, in celebrating the faith through the various festivals, and in forming and transmitting it from parents to children within the context of the home, is highly significant. In the course of its development, the identity of Israel as a nation, and the identity of the individuals, families and tribes that made up this nation, was primarily one of belonging, both to God and to a particular place. Throughout the Old Testament, the words 'You will be my people, and I will be your God' are linked with the words 'I will give you this land in which you are now a foreigner.' From the first covenant with Noah, through the great covenant with Abraham, with Isaac, and with Jacob, the overriding sense of belonging is to God, and the law given in Exodus and Deuteronomy is for individual and social behaviour that reflects that covenant.

Circumcision is the outward sign of the covenant: 'Every male among you shall be circumcised. You shall be circumcised in the flesh of your fore-skins, and it shall be a sign of the covenant between me and you' (Genesis 17.11 RSV). Through this sign, the covenant is both enacted and recalled. It is a deeply personal identification of the individual as a member of the covenant community. But that sense of belonging for the members of that covenant community was as a member of an extended family, a tribe, that belonged to God. From the time of Abraham onwards, the members of the new community of Israel belonged to God. Their sense of identity, of community, of law, and of family tradition was forged by the history of that covenant relationship. Put the other way around, it was God himself who formed the cohesion of the life of the tribe, the family and the individual.

But the single most telling statement on the place of the family as the central pivot around which the covenant relationship revolves is in the Passover celebration. Here, the story of God's liberation of his people from slavery in Egypt is celebrated not in the Temple, nor later in the synagogue, but in the home:

> 'And when you come to the land which the LORD will give you, as he has promised, you shall keep this service. And when your children say to you, "What do you mean by this service?", you shall say, "It is the sacrifice of the LORD's passover, for he passed over the houses of the people of Israel in Egypt, when he slew the Egyptians but spared our houses."' And the people bowed their heads and wor-shipped. Then the people of Israel went and did so; as the LORD had commanded Moses and Aaron, so they did. (Exodus 12.21–8 RSV)

The ritual itself remains a powerful symbol of liberation, particularly because it takes place in the family home and is celebrated by the family leader. And the fact that the specific inclusion of four questions asked by the youngest child remains a central part of the ritual to this day reinforces the dual role of the ritual as both worship and teaching. The family iden-tity as part of the covenant community who belong to God is established; God has brought them out of slavery to freedom. The responsibility of bringing up the children of the family in the faith and law of the covenant is restated. But it also brings the sacred into the heart of family life in a way that contemporary Christianity struggles to match. Here the most holy event in the history of the covenant community is celebrated by the family elders, in the family home, with the youngest child taking an important role in the ritual.

With the establishment of the new covenant in the death and resurrection of Christ and the subsequent dispensation of the Holy Spirit, the new Christian community began to reinterpret its understanding of covenant. Circumcision as a sign of the old covenant of law became a racial barrier that had to be overcome, rather than a symbol of belonging that could be celebrated. The response of faith of the uncircumcised Gentiles to Peter's preaching, recorded in Acts 10, followed by the gift of the Spirit, erased any lingering doubt in Peter's mind that this new covenant forged on the cross and proclaimed in the resurrection was for everyone, regardless of their background. The test of faith was the gift of the Holy Spirit, and the response to faith was baptism. Thus the transition from circumcision as the mark and sign of the old covenant, to baptism as the mark and sign of the new, was completed.

At the same time, the transition from the Passover to the eucharist as the central ritual of the Christian community, with its change of emphasis from liberation from slavery in Egypt to liberation from sin by the death and resurrection of Jesus, brought with it a profound change in our understanding of belonging.

This change in understanding begins with Jesus himself, as he calls the twelve away from their families and their domestic life to be his special companions. The twelve become symbolic of his new family: so much so, that when Jesus' relatives come to reason with him, he rejects them in favour of his disciples:

> While he was still speaking to the people, behold, his mother and his brothers stood outside, asking to speak to him. So one of the people there said to him, 'Look, your mother and brothers are standing outside, and they want to speak with you.' But he replied to the man who told him, 'Who is my mother, and who are my brothers?' And stretching out his hand toward his disciples, he said, 'Here are my mother and my brothers! For whoever does the will of my Father in heaven is my brother, and sister, and mother.' (Matthew 12.46–50 RSV)

The choice of place and company in the celebration of the Passover at the Last Supper appears to seal this transition. Jesus takes his disciples to the upper room, provided for him by an anonymous disciple, and there appears to reinterpret the Passover in terms of his own impending death. The unleavened bread is broken, and instead of setting aside the cup of wine in anticipation of the return of Elijah, it is passed round, signifying not only the completion of the prophecies, but the blood of the sacrificial lamb. Jesus appears to take the place of the Passover lamb, and the events of the next few days seal that interpretation into the central act of worship of the Christian Church.

It is not surprising, therefore, that instead of following the Jewish practice of celebrating Passover once a year in the home, the early Christian community met together rather more regularly to celebrate the common meal in remembrance of Jesus' death and resurrection and in anticipation of his imminent return. Human greed soon caused difficulties for such a gathering, as shown in the following passage from Paul, and one of the results of this was that the common meal was dropped, and the celebration of bread and wine became the central act of worship:

When you meet together, it is not the Lord's supper that you eat. For in eating, each one goes ahead with his own meal, and one is hungry and another is drunk. What! Do you not have houses to eat and drink in? Or do you despise the church of God and humiliate those who have nothing? What shall I say to you? Shall I commend you in this? No, I will not.' (1 Corinthians 11.20–2 RSV)

However, the transition of the central act of worship from the annual celebration of Passover in the family home to a more frequent celebration of the eucharist as a gathered community of faith meant that the individual Christian's focus of belonging inevitably shifted with it. That strong feeling of a direct covenant relationship between the family and God was replaced with a sense of the individual belonging primarily to a local community of faith – something that is evident today, and sometimes lamented by bishops and others, in that parishioners often appear to have no horizon beyond their parish church. At the same time, the strong sense of the sacred household, fostered by what we might well describe as the lay celebration of Passover in the family home, was replaced by a sense of the sacred community, or even the sacredness of the church or the altar. The process is further reinforced by the restriction of celebration to ordained clergy, where, for what most admit is a matter primarily of church order, the family is effectively deskilled in the celebration of the central act of Christian worship.

So the development of covenant theology has led, in many churches, to a theology of mission that is about persuading people to join, and a focus on seeking ways of encouraging them to come in. But those who belong by association are not 'fringe' members wanting to find a way in. On their own terms and by their own definition, they already belong. In the words of Alan Wilson, rector of Sandhurst: 'If I belong by association, and the Church is constantly prodding me to join this or that rota, or come to this or that service, it's really going to piss me off!' Any form of mission that treats those who belong by association as defective until signed up to participation is going to be not only counter-productive, but positively alienating for those associate members who experience it.

Perhaps their theology is less developed than that of many of our participant members, but it is possibly broader and sometimes more healthy. For those who belong by association, there is usually an unspoken and unformed assumption that God simply 'is'. God is in his (or her) heaven, and all's right with the world. And before we dismiss this as 'folk religion', we perhaps need to note the famous words of St Julian of Norwich: 'All shall be well, and all shall be well, and all manner of thing shall be well.' For associate members, membership of the covenant community is not an exclusive membership of a particular congregation, but a sense of belonging to God, no matter how vaguely this might be defined. And in this it might well be more true to the picture of belonging that comes to us from the old and new covenants than today's narrow emphasis on congregational participation.

By itself, and on its own terms, the theology of those who belong by association may well be more likely to be deist than Christian. Jesus may be 'a good man', or perhaps 'the best man who ever lived'. He is unlikely to be worshipped as God made flesh. There may also be more than a little 'Pelagianism'. Pelagius, a British monk, was responsible for the favourite British heresy, that individuals can save themselves by their own good deeds. How often, during the preparation for funerals, do those of us in pastoral ministry hear the sentiment that the deceased must be in heaven because of all the good things he or she did during his or her lifetime. Well, better that, perhaps, than hateful or cruel or criminal things! As Paul says, 'Indeed, when Gentiles, who do not have the law, do by nature things required by the law, they are a law for themselves, even though they do not have the law, since they show that the requirements of the law are written on their hearts, their consciences also bearing witness, and their thoughts now accusing, now even defending them' (Romans 2.14 RSV). For today's Church, it is probably those who belong by association, rather than those who reject a theistic view of life, who are in this respect the modern-day equivalent of Paul's 'Gentiles', who know instinctively what God requires of them.

But whatever theology is held, the point at issue is that for those who choose to belong by association, a choice has been made, and that choice is for Christ, in whatever way he is understood. The next small step in the pilgrimage has been made. I would strongly argue that the nature of this choice is no less valid, and no different in kind, than the choice made at a Billy Graham crusade, or the choice made at baptism or confirmation. The degree of choice, or at least the degree to which there is an awareness of making a choice, may be limited. It may simply be the unfocused decision to put 'Church of England' in the space on the form where it says 'Religion', or to put 'Catholic' there because that was the context of childhood religion. But even that small, unformed and often unconscious moment is a choice. If no other choice is made, then going back on it is entirely possible. But as least the first step has been taken. It would be a foolhardy person who could state categorically that such a choice had no meaning – yet, sadly, the denominational churches do not lack the foolhardy when it comes to making judgements about how others stand in relation to their creator.

Our concept of a covenant community needs to be extended to include all those who have made a choice for Christ – in whatever way that might be expressed – and at whatever level. It is the fact of choosing that is important. 'You will be my people and I will be your God' is translated into contemporary choice by 'I will choose to associate myself with Christ – or Christianity – or the Church of England – and not with secularism or any other form of religious commitment.' This, too, is a covenant relationship – modest maybe, and perhaps undefined, but nevertheless a choice over which the angels are no doubt rejoicing.

To suppose otherwise is to believe what is perhaps the most pervasive of modern heresies. It is not the Pelagianism of those who 'did it my way', who believe that salvation can be earned by good works. That heresy is sometimes fostered by organizations such as the Royal British Legion and the Freemasons. It is rather the heresy, beloved by many in both the Evangelical and Catholic traditions, that salvation comes only by holding the 'correct' doctrine. How that doctrine is defined will vary, but all too often this heresy gives voice to the feeling that to be saved, you have to believe the same things as 'us'. It probably begins with a basic insecurity, because to accept as 'saved' those who believe radically different things about God is to accept that one's own beliefs may not be quite as central to salvation as one might wish. I call this the heresy of salvation by correct doctrine, and it infects too many of our churches. It is in essence a kind of fundamentalism, where those who do not agree with 'us' are at best suspect, and at worst, excommunicated. It is an irony that those who are most likely to affirm the traditional evangelical understanding that salvation is a gift of grace, and comes by faith alone, are often whose who are most tempted to express this heresy in their preaching and ecclesiology by demanding adherence to this or that particular doctrine.

It takes almost as many forms as there are churches. One congregation may insist that its members hold to certain doctrines on glossolalia – and if you don't speak in tongues, then you are suspect. Another may take the opposite view. Yet another may require acceptance of the real presence of Christ in the bread and wine of the eucharist – and yet another may reject that doctrine with equal vehemence. The point is that all these communities will reject as 'unsound' anyone who holds a different theological interpretation. And with that rejection comes the sense that those who hold a different doctrine are 'unsound', which leads all too easily to 'unsaved'. Thus one of the most fundamental of Christian beliefs, that anyone who turns to Christ in repentance and faith is justified by that faith, is negated – often on very spurious grounds.

The Australian Community leader Dave Andrews has helpfully used the language of sociology to define and unpack this narrow approach to Christianity. He calls this traditional Christian approach 'closed set Christianity' (Andrews 1999). He describes how people belonging to a particular 'closed set' use particular beliefs and behaviours to define membership of that set. People can be part of the 'in' set by subscribing to certain beliefs and behaviours – such as, for example, 'submitting to the authority of Scripture' or 'recognizing the real presence of Christ in the Eucharist'. People who don't are not part of, and can never be part of, this particular set. It is, quite literally, a closed set. It is not open to anyone, but only to those who subscribe to the beliefs, values and behaviours of that particular set. Problems arise when an 'insider', a member of the closed set, either rejects or is discovered not to subscribe to one of the defining beliefs or behaviours of the set. That person then either leaves, or is 'excommunicated' by the members of, that particular set.

It is by defining these particular beliefs, values and behaviours that members of 'closed set' Christianity gain their identity. Security comes from knowing that one is an insider, a member of the 'confessing' group. Specific forms of language become a badge of membership; particular ways of behaving become tokens of belonging.

I well remember this totemic use of both language and behaviour from my student days. During the early 1970s, the sectarian problems in Northern Ireland and their increasingly negative effect on Christian witness had become a matter of conscience for some of us. A group of students organized a scheme whereby children from different sectarian locations were taken by train from Northern Ireland to so-called 'neutral' territory in the South, and given a two-week holiday. As students, we ran this

'Northern Ireland Children's Holiday Scheme' with the purpose not only of giving the children a holiday away from the tensions and violence of their streets, but of allowing them to mix with children from different 'closed set' communities, hopefully to lay the groundwork for future reconciliation. It was a difficult thing to negotiate, because we were only too aware that the shadowy 'community leaders' with whom we were negotiating may well have been (and probably were) part of the paramilitary group who would have the final say on whether children from 'their' community would be allowed to take part. I have always suspected that perhaps the greater bravery in those troubled times was not ours (although it felt scary at the time) but that of those community leaders, who were clearly taking considerable risks in allowing 'their' children to meet with the hated enemy.

The first problem we encountered was that the train bringing the children from Northern Ireland itself became a series of 'closed set' communities. Catholic children congregated in one carriage, and Protestant children in another. Any child wishing to pass from one carriage to the other was challenged at the doorway by the children stationed at the entrance to the carriage. 'Say the "Hail Mary"' was the challenge from the Catholic group. 'Say the Lord's Prayer' was the challenge from the Protestants. This was 'closed set' Christianity at its worst, a breeding ground for suspicion, hatred and possible violence. As student leaders, we were often challenged in the first few days as to whether we were 'Prod' or 'Cath'lik'. Our line was quite clear. We were neither. We were simply 'Christian'. Thus we attempted to avoid reinforcing the closed set mentality, and to provide a context within which the children could, in their own time, meet each other across the barriers of sectarianism. I shall never forget the generosity of the Catholic Benedictine monks of Clongowswood who allowed us to use their school for successive holidays. The children were not always kind to those buildings, and sometimes the damage was more than superficial. But the rewards were considerable. Every day, the monks would celebrate a eucharist for us, and everyone was invited. Towards the end of the two weeks, considerable numbers of Protestant children would creep in to the back of the chapel simply to observe the mass. It was a remarkable time, and I pray that it might have made some small contribution to the peace initiative that came nearly thirty years later.

The language and definitions that Andrews uses are those of sociology, but I would argue that the problem he is defining is not a sociological problem, but a theological one: in the language of sociology, he is describing the essence of a heresy. And the heresy he is describing is the heresy of salvation by correct doctrine. It is this theology that is used to deny the often unconscious choice made by those who belong by association – the choice for, rather than against, Christ. For those who make even the smallest internal choice are affirming a choice for God and for Christ. The result of this combination of closed set thinking and narrow theology is to drive fracture lines of division through the Christian community. But worse, it creates a climate in which those who belong by association are excluded.

The theologian Robert Brinsmead comments on the serious consequences of maintaining these boundaries:

> Religion draws lines of demarcation through the human race. The chosen people are distinguished from the unchosen, insiders from outsiders, clean from unclean, believers from unbelievers, the enlightened from the unenlightened. People who live within separate barriers cannot effectively communicate. What is orthodoxy to one group, is blasphemy to another[.] (Brinsmead 1989: 5)

Brinsmead begs us to recognize that it is religious devotees such as ourselves, devoted to our various, mutually exclusive 'bounded sets', that are directly, or indirectly, 'moving millions towards a jihad of violence everywhere from Ireland to Lebanon, and from Bosnia to India!', and that

> If we want it to be otherwise, we need to find another way of defining our faith that is not so defensive; another way of affirming our faith that is not so aggressive; a way of comprehending our faith that is true, but doesn't pretend to have a monopoly on truth; and a way of interpreting our faith that is inclusive, not exclusive, of all that is good and healthy and holy and right in other cultures, traditions and religions. (Brinsmead 1989: 6–7)

Many Christians would rejoice at this straightforward rejection of the traditional 'closed set', or possibly 'closed mind', Christianity. This is not because it is potentially as dangerous as Brinsmead suggests: though it may well be, as fundamentalist-inspired terrorism attests; nor because it divides us into ever more fractured sets, though it obviously does. It is rejected because it denies the biblical theology of salvation by faith in Christ alone, and substitutes for faith a particular set of doctrines – doctrines that can be, and often are, boiled down to mere slogans, or mere slogans dressed up as doctrines.

Andrews defines an alternative paradigm which he calls 'centred set Christi-anarchy'. But there is really little need for it to be anarchic – it is a form of Christian self-understanding that is more Johannine, or possibly more Benedictine, than anarchic in its approach.

According to the centred set perspective, a set is defined by a 'centre', which is free, and cannot ever be enclosed, least of all by the experts. From this perspective, a set of people who have a connection to Christ show they are part of the set, not by choosing to subscribe to certain beliefs and behaviours within certain boundaries, but by choosing to overcome any boundary of belief or behaviour that might prevent them from moving towards the free, beautiful, compassionate spirit of Christ, which they have made the centre of their lives.

'Conversion' in the language of those who subscribe to centred set Christianity is not a matter of embracing any particular doctrines, behaviours or beliefs; rather, it is a matter of beginning a journey towards Christ – whether he is known by that name or by another – and of beginning to judge our own lives, our own standards and behaviours, in the light of that non-judgemental love that shines from the words and person of Jesus. We have no means of judging others, because if we are walking alongside friends who have started in different places and have arrived from different directions, we have no way of knowing where anyone other than ourselves stands in relation to God. It is the 'conversio morem' of St Benedict's rule, the lifetime taken to learn obedience and love by walking alongside others in a common pilgrimage of exploration.

For those who belong to a closed set, it is not just 'easy' to judge where people stand, who is 'in' and who is 'out'; it is a required part of belonging itself.

Yet the Gospels show that being saved is not a matter of uniform participation in a cult community. Otherwise the prostitutes would be far below the Pharisees in the pecking order of the Kingdom. Rather it is a matter of responding to the call of God, wherever and however it may be heard. For one, it may be a matter of stopping to care for the injured man on the road to Jericho. For another, it may be the recognition that his father's pigs are fed better than he is. Or again, it may be the emotional response of pouring the most expensive perfume on the feet of our Lord. If there is one thing that is clear from the Gospels, it is that Jesus' call is different for each one of us. He was not interested in demanding doctrinal uniformity, but in calling us to become a community of diversity, celebrating God's call in whatever way it might be experienced. His expectations were not rigid standards, but a response to a call that is as individual as the individuals who can respond.

So far, I have deliberately set up an opposition between 'centred set' and 'closed set' Christianity. But in practice, it is not that simple. There are plenty of people who are participant members of closed set churches who hold happily, and confidently, to a centre set theology without being attacked or excommunicated by their fellow-members. They very often form the bridges that allow others to move out of a narrow, restrictive understanding of their faith that would otherwise have stopped them growing, or even possibly led them to reject Christianity as a way of seeing the world as sacred.

Those who belong to our churches by association rather than by participation are natural centre set Christians. They are not willing to be 'pasteurized', as one friend of mine eloquently put it. They see the churches as a resource, perhaps only one resource among many, for their own spiritual journey. They will use the Church when they need it, and forget it when they don't. They will come at Christmas, or maybe not, depending on their needs and the needs of those around them. They may seek out a priest should they feel the need for one, or visit a church during the week to light a candle or say a prayer. They are not willing to see their faith as a separate entity from their family or their work – it will be part and parcel of the whole. Thus, any notion of joining a church as a prerequisite to salvation will be alien to them. For our associate members, salvation is seen in wholistic terms – as the proper balance of family and working life with the life of the spirit. Of course, this is to articulate what may be an inarticulate, or even inarticulable, mindset. For our associate members, it may simply be a matter of feeling uncomfortable being 'pasteurized'.

And who is to blame if their theology is unformed? How much of our resources have been spent on informing their faith? Have we not focused the vast majority of our financial, educational and communication resources on those who belong by participation? We need to learn once again how to become servants. A servant church is not simply a church that looks after its own members better; it is a church that is there for others, for those outside itself, for those who claim membership but who rarely come. It is a church that is happy to baptize, to marry, to bury and above all to celebrate those who say 'I am Church of England' even if they last went to a church before Mattins was first said.

Chapter 5

Believing What?

The overriding question raised by the previous chapters is simply this: if believing is belonging, then what kind of belief qualifies you for belonging? Does it matter what you believe? Will any kind of belief 'do' for belonging, or is there still a doctrinal demand to be made on those who choose to associate with the Christian church, rather than become participant members?

And the answer must surely be that it matters very much; it is critically important. Because, ultimately, belief needs to be related in some way to reality. The person who believes (for example) that God is simply a piece of cream cheese may be harmless, but is still a very long way from reality. The terrorist who believes that God has called him to fly an aircraft loaded with innocent passengers into the World Trade Center may be passionately committed to his faith, but is nonetheless a long way from reality in his understanding about God, from the religion he believes he is acting upon, and from the most fundamental of all beliefs, the belief in the sacredness of all human life. He is certainly not harmless.

So does it matter what you believe? Absolutely. The search for truth is at the heart of the gospel. And will anything do? No. Clearly the search for truth takes us on a pilgrimage of faith, where the search for an authentic experience of the divine mystery leads us to exclude false, misleading or just plain bad religious understanding and practice. Faith is not an irrational acceptance of the illogical or impossible. It is, at heart, a way, the most satisfying way, of making sense of reality because reality, for the Christian, is truth, and truth reveals God's creative, forgiving energy and love.

Thus the search for reality, for truth, for authenticity, is an important test of a genuine religious pilgrimage. Christians should not be afraid of the enquiring mind: we should celebrate it, even when the search takes us into uncomfortable territory. If God is at the heart of reality, then any search for truth will inevitably take us nearer to the heart of the sacred. The difficulty experienced by so many Christians, particularly those who have worshipped and lived within a closed set congregation, is that many of their fellow Christians don't see it like this. For them, Christianity is not about an exploration into truth; it's about holding firm to a fixed set of beliefs. Any deviation from this set creates a crisis of belonging, and Christian history is littered with the casualties that inevitably result. The debate at the end of the nineteenth century about the origin of the human species, for example, did enormous damage to the relationship between science and the sacred precisely because the Christians involved either didn't understand that the search for scientific truth is a pilgrimage toward God's reality, or rejected the conclusions of that search because they couldn't reconcile them with the framework of beliefs that they felt their religion required them to defend. Instead of seeing scientific exploration as part of the sacredly inspired search for truth, it was seen (and still is in some parts of the Church) as a threat to a closed set church and the closed mind of an individual.

But is this inability to embrace difference and change a spiritual problem, or is it perhaps more of a health problem? The ability to live with those who disagree with you has at least as much to do with your level of emotional maturity as it does your spiritual maturity; in fact, the two may be closely linked.

Each of us grows up with a particular level of emotional health, formed by the kind of relationships we experienced in childhood. At the lower end of the health spectrum is the controlling family, where completely fixed views about 'the other' are used to create a fragile sense of security within the family. Such families maintain their sense of identity and security by denigrating those who differ from them. Thus a neighbour whose child aspires to college or university may represent a threat to their own security, and such behaviour will be criticized as being 'posh' or 'above their station' (to use an old-fashioned phrase). Rather than celebrate diversity, such families will maintain their identity and sense of security by criticizing it. 'Be like me' is the motto, rather than 'Be yourself.' When this touches religious issues, it becomes potentially dangerous. 'Be like me' becomes 'Believe what I believe,' or even 'In this street we are all good Protestants, or Catholics, or whatever.' In families with a low level of emotional health, there will be a keen sense of belonging and security reinforced by rigidly enforced shared values, but a very low tolerance shown towards those who differ.

In such a family, love is often conditional. You are loved not for who you are, but for what you do and how you do it. Behaviour changes result in the withdrawal of love, and this has the effect of reinforcing the insecurity that lies at the heart of such controlling behaviour, and therefore of making the child's sense of security dependent on holding a particular narrow set of beliefs or values.

This will inevitably be coupled with a fairly low level of insight into the effects of such rigidity on the family itself. Children will find it almost impossible to break out of the family's value set without experiencing pain, and so they unconsciously seek ways to avoid that pain. At school, this will probably manifest itself in truculence, or confusion, because one of the aims of education is to help children grow in emotional maturity, and to help them discover and value the variety of human experience. So, faced with a challenge to their security, such children will probably rebel. At best, they will face severe confusion. In church, this will probably manifest itself in doctrinal rigidity. Those young adults who have moved away from homes with a fairly low level of emotional health without having made much of an emotional transition through school will naturally seek out communities where security is created through dogmatic belief systems. Some may be attracted to fundamentalist political parties; others to the more fundamentalist churches; some will be attracted to a combination of both. They will not recognize this as an issue to do with emotional health, but will express it in terms of right and wrong religious (or political) belief. Any kind of statement that expresses any form of provisionality – 'This explanation seems to fit my own perception and spiritual journey for now' – will be rejected as unspiritual or doctrinally deficient. And there will be little expectation of doctrinal change or growth, because that would challenge their individual sense of security. It would be, quite literally, frightening.

I am not arguing that this rigid, controlling and narrow form of Christian believing is not Christian, nor that such belief is outside Christianity, any more than I would argue that a controlling husband or wife is less 'married' simply because he or she has some growing to do. But very often, the most essential part of becoming holy is the pilgrimage from certainty to uncertainty, the ability to embrace the provisionality of our current understanding, allowing for the possibility that others may be right and we may be wrong. It is precisely this kind of spirituality that enables others to explore their own faith by giving them the freedom to differ. What I am arguing for is a holistic understanding of spiritual health; the recognition that one of the marks of spiritual and emotional maturity is the ability to walk alongside those with whom we disagree while allowing them to be different.

At the other end of the emotional spectrum to this rigid form of believing are those who grow up in a set of relationships that are secure because love is not dependent on behaviour or values, but rather the child is loved for him- or herself. An outsider coming into a family with a high level of emotional health will experience a high energy level, where each member is fully occupied in being themselves, while supporting the other members of the family in being themselves as well. It can, to the outsider, appear almost chaotic, and will contrast starkly with the dull, blocked energy of the family expressing a low level of emotional health. For those growing up in emotionally healthy families, because love is unconditional, there can at first appear to be a kind of arrogance. Comments will be casually expressed and casually received in such families that would lead to outrage in other families. But such families are exciting to be with. They 'bring out the best' in you, and help you feel liberated. Above all, they foster a sense of individual responsibility for behaviour, where in other families the responsibility is either rejected – 'they made me do it' – or used as a weapon of control.

This kind of emotional health almost inevitably carries with it a fair degree of insight into the behaviour and beliefs of others, which in itself can be threatening to those who are not at that level of health. At school, it will be expressed in questioning, and possibly in questioning the rules and values of the school itself. In church, it will result in an openness to people of other faiths and belief systems, and as such can be highly threatening to those whose doctrinal position is formed by their need for security, rather than by their discovery of the spiritual.

The question of the level of emotional health becomes even more interesting when you realize that communities and institutions can also exhibit various levels of collective emotional maturity. They have a personality that may be high, or low, on the scale of emotional health. If someone with a very different level of emotional health joins such a community, it can create considerable difficulties. For example, someone who brings with them a fairly low level of emotional health is going to find membership of a church which expresses a high level of health very threatening. They will feel insecure, and will almost certainly blame the church itself. Equally, someone with a high level of emotional health will not feel comfortable in a church where a fairly low level is expressed. He or she may express views regarded by the church members as almost heretical, and will very probably tolerate beliefs and behaviours that are inimical to the church itself. His or her expressions of Christian commitment will be questioned, and often doubted, possibly even by the minister concerned.

This, of course, raises the question of how to move a church with a low level of emotional health higher up the scale. This cannot be achieved by theological discussion – such discussion will quickly become a test of orthodoxy – but through experiential contact with people at slightly higher levels of emotional health. The work can best be done not by concentrating on areas of potential religious conflict, but in terms of behavioural acceptance. Travel is often a way of breaking out of an unhealthy emotional context, and the benefit of the group pilgrimage may be more that it brings church members into fairly constant contact with those of higher emotional maturity than that it teaches them about the physical geography or history of their faith. Such work is the subject of a different book, but it needs to be recognized that if believing is belonging, the nature of that belief may be conditioned as much by emotional health as by spiritual maturity, and thus the commitment to belonging may change for reasons quite unconnected with spirituality. Growing may be emotional, and may lead directly out the door of the church as a healthy exploration of difference begins. Such 'leaving' may be the first steps of a pilgrimage to deeper understanding, even if it means that participant membership gives way to associate membership.

But at what level does a Christian understanding have to be present in order for an individual to claim authentic membership of the Church? For example, the demand made by Islam on those who wish to belong is relatively simple: you have to believe that there is only one God, Allah, who created the entire universe, and that Muhammad is his final messenger on earth. If you recite this, with total sincerity, in front of two witnesses, you have become a Muslim. There is no demand for membership of a mosque; no doctrinal tests; no rite of initiation. Simply a public declaration of belief in front of two witnesses. Traditional Christian understanding has been that baptism is the entry point of Christianity, yet this too raises a question. Baptism is the outward and visible sign of an internal commitment. Presumably the internal decision precedes the act of baptism – sometimes by many years. That internal decision may be conscious, but it is more likely to be an unconscious recognition of the reality of the sacred that slowly and imperceptibly moves into consciousness, probably before the individual him- or herself is aware of it. Or it may happen the other way around. Baptism may be the starting point of the pilgrimage of faith, and any sense of intellectual or emotional commitment to Christ may be much further down the road. The equivalent phrase, 'I turn to Christ, I repent of my sins, I renounce evil', may well be the core statement of Christian belonging.

What I am arguing for is a theology that is bigger than the Church; that breaks down the walls of our denominational exclusivity; and above all, one that recognizes those who belong by association as a full part of our Christian community and not merely potential participant members of congregations. One starting point, as I have already argued, is the recognition of the sacredness of creation, and the demands that such a recognition makes on our behaviour. But we need to go further if our understanding is to be specifically Christian. We need to recognize that the cross and the resurrection are not simply at the heart of the Church and its worship, or even at the heart of Christian belief. They are written into the fabric of the universe. They do not achieve significance at the moment we are baptized, but at the moment we are born, whether or not we are born into a family of faith. Our world, our universe, is one where the principles of the cross and the resurrection are as fundamental to its working as the law of gravity, or the reality of falling in love. They are written through it as clearly as the words through a stick of Brighton rock. So clearly are they part of the way the world is that they should be seen as a spiritual principle as central to our understanding as time or matter. You do not have to be a member of a church, or even a committed Christian, to experience the reality of the relationship between sacrifice and resurrection.

This is not just romantic wish-fulfilment: it can be demonstrated as clearly as the law of universal gravitation. For example, a young man in a crowded tube train sees an elderly woman struggle through the doors, and in a simple act of generosity gives up his seat. This may be a very small matter for the young man – it may not even register to him that he is making any kind of sacrifice, but the choice he has made to forgo the comfort of his seat out of consideration for the other person is a choice that is linked to the cross, and the results it brings are just as surely linked to the resurrection. The woman may not recognize the act as anything more than one of simple kindness; her experience of refreshment, or relief, or renewal, may not extend beyond a short physical relief. But it is in the relationship between the two actions – a choice to 'give up' in favour of the 'other', and the result of that 'giving up' for the 'other' – that the universal principle of cross and resurrection is found.

This is not merely human kindness, though of course human kindness is forged from acts such as these. It is a reflection of the reality of the cross and the resurrection, the same reality that shines from the Gospels, because it is not simply a subjective reality to those who believe; it is a concrete, objective reality to that is part of the way things are, just as gravity or light are part of the fabric of our universe. It is the point at which the sacred meets everyday life, wherever that is, and however it is contextualized.

If this simple, and minor, example begins our exploration into the way the world is, it doesn't end it. Take, for example, the current difficulties in Northern Ireland, or in any of the apparently immovable conflicts around the world. The only possible way towards resolution is when one side or the other is prepared to give up a central demand or ambition, to say to the other, 'I will sacrifice this or that principle so that we can move towards peace.' The sacrifices may proceed agonizingly slowly, each small movement needing to be matched by the other. They may be light-years away from the absolute and total abandonment of demands in which the Christ embraces the will of our Father and goes to the cross. But these small sacrifices are, none the less, a reflection of the cross. And they result, none the less, in a reflection of the light and peace of the empty tomb and the joy of the first Easter morning.

And so the young man who gives up his seat on the Underground, or the terrorist who gives up some small demand in order to move towards peace, both reflect the face of Christ on the cross.

As I have said, seen from a 'closed set' perspective, these actions are merely human kindness, and nothing to do with the Church. Yet from the perspective of 'centred set' faith, they reflect a central reality of Christianity – that all our actions, all our understanding, are either moving towards or away from the heart of God, whether or not we make an explicit statement of faith or even whether we recognize the fact.

These actions become small 'defining moments' because each of the people concerned has made a choice – they have chosen to give up something of themselves – in order to bring refreshment, healing, peace, to the other. They may not see their actions in religious terms, and might strongly reject any religious, let alone Christian, interpretation. That does not matter. What matters is that the link is there as objectively and clearly as the space between Good Friday and Easter. This is the 'deeper magic' that C.S. Lewis refers to in *The Lion, the Witch and the Wardrobe*. It is what authenticates our believing, and makes it distinctively Christian. God is not a stranger to human activity, welcomed in only when we make a conscious decision to do so. He is present in the lives and actions of all who seek goodness, kindness, redemption or hope. And neither are we a people who follow a book of religious rules; or rather, if we do begin by following the rules we soon discover that they lead us beyond them to something much greater and more dynamic – to the Spirit of God himself. We follow the one who gave his life for us on the cross, and who was raised on the first Easter morning. We listen to the one who taught us to reach out in love to our enemy; to give to those in need, measuring our giving not by the level of our resources but by the level of their need. Not only do we allow prayer to transform our mind, but in listening to the one that Jesus called 'Abba, Father', we learn to respond in obedience to the 'irrational' promptings of the Spirit, to live more and more within the loving embrace of his will.

Again, I am not suggesting that those who seek to live within the 'rules' are somehow less Christian than those who simply follow the freedom and inspiration of the Spirit. This is an old argument that caused plenty of division in the early Church, and it is wrong. Part of our Christian pilgrimage is to learn obedience to the will of Christ. What I am saying, however, is that the rules point beyond themselves to the will of the one who was prepared to break them in the name of love. Jesus broke plenty of religious rules. He healed people on the Sabbath. He picked ears of corn and ate them on the Sabbath. He had the temerity to rise from the dead after the religious leaders had ensured his death. Again, I emphasize that I am not arguing for a deliberate rejection of rules, any more than I would advise a trainee pilot to throw away the flight manual and try to fly by instinct. Both individuals and communities need clear boundaries within which to learn how to live the life of non-judgemental love, just as the trainee pilot needs the flight manual to learn how to fly correctly. But there has to come a time when flying becomes a joyous, instinctive act; and in a similar way, there has to be a transition from a faith governed by 'rules' to one where those rules give way to the guidance of the Spirit of God himself.

This is the kind of believing that ultimately makes faith authentic. It is the 'what' of Christian belief. And, sadly, it is often the kind of faith that people come to our churches to find, but leave having failed to find it. It is one of the depressing statistics of contemporary churchgoing that considerable numbers of people are leaving the Church not because they have lost their faith, but because traditional churchgoing does not meet the demands of their faith. There are many who still participate, but do so not out of a sense of challenge or excitement, but from a sense of duty or loyalty. For them, believing, not belonging, is the more authentic expression of the Kingdom.

Professor Leslie J. Francis, in his Essex Hall Lecture as early as 1994, reports on the interim findings from the Young People, Religion and Values Today research project. In this report, Professor Francis identifies, 'for the sake of brevity', three distinct groups of young people: 'unbelievers', 'believers-without-belonging', and 'practising believers'. He says: 'More than two fifths (44%) of the believers-without-belonging' report that they never pray. More than two thirds (69%) report that they never read the Bible. More than nine-tenths (92%) report that they never say grace before meals. Believing-without-belonging seems, therefore, to imply the acceptance of the existence of God, without developing a personal response to that God' (Francis 1994: 9). But this seems a curious conclusion to draw from the data. If saying grace before meals is the criterion on which to base the conclusion, I would agree; but it is a weak criterion. The study actually found that 56 per cent of young people who believe without belonging did admit to praying. It found that 31 per cent had read the Bible at some point. This seems to me to give a different picture, one where there is some kind of direct and personal response, even if it is weak and less defined than in those Francis labels 'practising believers'. When you look at the findings of the same study in relation to Christian belief, far from confirming his rather negative conclusions, they appear to contradict them. Seventy per cent of those who believe without belonging accepted that Jesus Christ is the Son of God; 51 per cent believe that Jesus really rose from the dead; and 52 per cent believed in life after death. It would be interesting to redo the research today; in cultural terms, 1994 is a long time ago and youth culture has changed dramatically. I suspect we might well find a rise in the number of young people who are prepared to own a specific spirituality, and that a much larger percentage would own non-Christian, or even pagan, beliefs.

So what kind of Church is needed to enable us to celebrate the natural spirituality of the twenty-first century? Strangely enough, the Anglican Church is ideally placed to support those who belong by association. It is an inclusive church, welcoming all who belong to a particular geographical area. It is particularly open to a centred set perspective, because it makes few or no demands for membership beyond a desire to participate. It has room for people of all backgrounds and levels of education. But it has increasingly suffered from a drift to a 'closed set' theology, partly because it has sometimes been tempted to lose its nerve in the face of the massive apparent growth among the 'closed set' denominations. It needs to trust its purpose and recover its vision.

So how can we transform our present, essentially medieval, church system into something that relates better to our future culture, and that educates and informs the spirituality of both participant and associate members? How do we create the kind of environment that educates and informs that natural spirituality, and allows it the freedom of exploration as well as the discipline of transformation? Does the local church set itself against popular culture and require its members, both participant and associate, to conform to a new dynamic, and if so, what should that dynamic be? Or does it follow the trends of popular culture, using its forms of art, of music, of media and of relationships to convey the values of the Kingdom? One thing is certain: there is almost overwhelming evidence that simply doing better what we have done in the past is not going to be enough. The twentieth century, with its universal education and its massive shift to interconnectedness and disintermediation, has effectively changed the shape of the Church for good. We may not yet have fully realized it, but we cannot expect models of the Church that are failing to satisfy the spiritual needs of our community to work simply by making them run better. A differently shaped Church is needed.

Chapter 6

The Church in Transformation

I believe in getting into hot water; it keeps you clean.
G. K. Chesterton

When we lose the energy and drive to do something, we either abandon it or put in place structures to maintain the initiative so that our real interests and energy can be diverted elsewhere. The assumption is that even if we don't have the interest or energy to maintain the initiative, others will. But what if we are not the only ones losing interest? There are those who will abandon the Church when they lose the energy to participate because they have no ties to it. There are many who remain, but who simply create structures that replace their initial energy. One key question for today's Church is whether the structures we have are there because we believe in them, or because they provide a substitute for energy we no longer have – they are there to perpetuate something we no longer believe in. Eventually, the structures that we have created implode if no one believes any longer that they are useful. For example, evensong as a full choral service has all but disappeared from most parish churches. And with our culture and values changing all around us, we have to find new ways of creating sacred communities that meet the needs of those who no longer want to be part of a tradition rooted in the sixteenth century.

It was the religious community, not the parish system, that converted England from its pagan practice during what we used to call the Dark Ages. Small groups of people who had committed their whole lives to prayer, to study and to serving their local communities came together under a common rule of life to develop an alternative society – a model of living that reflected both the values and the lifestyle of the kingdom of God. They were the new radicals for their age; they took the values of the gospel, supported by the best education, and applied them not only to prayer and study, but to compassion and service. By the twelfth century, the monasteries and religious communities had become the spiritual powerhouse for the education, healing and conversion of England.

History may have judged them harshly, and they may well have been in need of reform, but the dissolution of the monasteries several hundred years later was possibly the single most effective act of spiritual vandalism committed by the state in the history of English Christianity. It robbed the nation, and therefore the parish churches, of their points of spiritual reference, of their centres of learning, and of their places of hospitality and retreat. Like many in today's Church, there were plenty of monks and nuns at the time of the Dissolution who had lost their vision. One abbot, reflecting on the loss of his monastery, is reputed to have said: 'I lost my abbot's heart ten years before I lost my abbot's hat.' But that loss of heart and vision was, and is today, nothing more or less than the need for transformation from one culture to another of a vision for religious communities that can engage with the needs of the nation. The transformation of the local parish church into a new form of religious community has been going on for many years.

It was not the monastic system itself that had failed, but rather the ability of that system to change and adapt to a new culture. The fortress mentality necessary to survive the Dark Ages that had forged the enclosed orders had given way to a much more open society, one of trade and commerce, and because the old monastic system was unable to engage effectively with the changes, its members lost heart. They knew deep down that something was wrong, but were unable to adapt. The parish system, which had grown up alongside the monastic communities, was left to bear the full weight of mission that it was not properly designed for.

You only have to look at the average parish church today to see how much it is still based on its monastic roots. The liturgies of matins and evensong, transformed more recently into family services or evening worship, are conflations of the monastic hours. Prime, terce, sext and none are combined into a single morning office; Evensong and Compline to a single evening office. Even the physical layout of the average parish church speaks of its monastic pattern: the choir was not intended for singers in Victorian costumes, but for monks and nuns singing the offices. The pattern of the daily offices is monastic in origin. Even the concept of the parish church as the oratory of the geographical parish is monastic; the vicar, like the abbot, calls his community to worship each day, and the monastic assumption that the first duty of the faithful is to attend the offices, the worship of the oratory, remains at the heart of parish life. Yet of the two foundational principles that made the parish system work, establishment and *episcope*, only one is fully acknowledged today.

The parish system can only survive today as an effective system of mission if there is a critical mass of the population who support it, and if the central ideas that drive it are both understood and maintained. It is, essentially, a system for administering Christendom, but if Christendom disappears, then it is fatally weakened. The parish system is based on two central ideas. The first is to do with the monarch, the second with the bishop, and the roots of both can be traced back to the adoption by the medieval monarchs of an essentially Roman method of administration. The concept of a Christian kingdom, where the monarch has both spiritual and temporal care of his subjects, lies at the heart of the parish system, and is the essence of Establishment. The three great duties of a Christian monarch were, first, to provide an army to protect the external security of his or her subjects, next, to look after their spiritual well-being, and third, to provide for their temporal needs by encouraging trade and commerce as well as looking after the needy, the poor and the sick. The Church was never restricted to a believing congregation; under the monarch it was charged with both spiritual care and much of the task of the relief of the poor and the sick. The bishops were part of the state mechanism, not through corruption, but simply because they had a job to do that was integral to the health and well-being of the nation. Parishes became the means of administering this model of Christendom; they were not merely centres for prayer and worship, but for the relief of poverty and sickness. Charitable giving was a practical necessity as well as a spiritual duty. The burial of the dead was also a Christian duty, and so the Church effectively became the nation's burial authority.

The Servant Church: Schools and Education

In the late eighteenth and early nineteenth century, education was increasingly seen as the means of escape from poverty and disease, and so the Church took the lead in the movement for universal education. Sunday schools were started, the first in 1789, not as a means of providing religious instruction to the children of Church members, but as a way of providing basic education for members of the parish. In 1811 the National Society for Promoting the Education of the Poor in the Principles of the Established Church was set up by the Church of England to provide schools. It was, once again, an example of engagement with the needs of the community that drove the mission of the Church. If you follow the marriage registers of the average parish church in any medium-sized town from the beginning of the nineteenth century through to the end, you will see a remarkable change taking place. Early in that century, few people could write their names. Most of the women, and a large proportion of the men, would sign the registers not with their name but with their mark. Often it was an 'X', witnessed by someone who could affirm that the maker of 'Sarah, her mark' was who she said she was. Yet by the late 1800s, the mark has all but died out. Careful, copper-plate handwriting fills the marriage registers from about the 1880s.

What brought about this change? First, the Sunday school movement, with its emphasis on teaching the children of the parish the basics of reading, writing and arithmetic. Then, as the Church lobbied for universal education, land and money was given, often by the lord of the manor or his equivalent, to allow the Church to build a parish school and employ a teacher. Sunday schools became parish schools. And as the effectiveness of this form of mission was proved, so the state came alongside and provided the resources to make this education truly universal. It was only in 1876 that Parliament first required parents to send their children to school, and it was only in the 1890s that a series of Education Acts brought free education to the majority of our children.

This is simply one, fairly recent, example of how the parish system of administration, based on the medieval concept of the Church as the provider of both spiritual and temporal welfare, helped it engage with those who belonged both by participation and by association. The stories of the Bible, often reflected in medieval paintings and Victorian stained glass, were used as the teaching material. This formed the almost universal world-view of the working people, who would know the accounts of Adam and Eve, of Jonah and the whale, of Jesus feeding the five thousand, and the crucifixion and resurrection, because education and religious knowledge almost always came from the same source. Although the state progressively took on much of the responsibility of education, filling in the geographical gaps in schooling by building parish schools, the Church historically had the largest say in primary education until well after the First World War, and continues to have a very large presence in primary education to this day. In Oxfordshire, for example, more than 50 per cent of the primary schools are still Church of England aided or controlled.

In the survey on the Lord's Prayer carried out for the Archbishops' Millennium Advisory Group, the Gallup organization asked a sample of the population if they knew it, and if they did, where they had learned it. By far the largest number of people had learned it not in Church, nor from their parents or grandparents, but at school. And the point at which that knowledge began to drop off coincides with the point at which the Church introduced liturgical reforms. Of course, more research would be needed to prove a causal relationship, but it may well be significant that schools stopped teaching it at almost exactly the same time that the Church changed the language.

Secularization and Loss of Direction

But with the success of education came the first seeds of the failure of the parish system. It was both good and necessary that the government progressively funded from taxation the role of education, health, care for the poor, and most of the other caring functions that the Church had performed from medieval times. Taxes are, after all, one of the most important means of making our charitable giving both fair and universal. But with the growth of state provision came the growth of secularism, which reached its peak in the 1960s and 1970s. The Church, which until the Second World War had been deeply integrated into the life of the community at just about every level, from health care to education, from relief of poverty to the magistry, had become isolated. While the National Society, together with diocesan boards of education, continued to play a major role in education, they became increasingly secularized; by the 1990s it was often difficult to see any overt Christian practice in Church schools, apart from attendance by the local vicar at school assemblies and his (and latterly her) minority membership of the governing body. The imposition of a national curriculum by a commercially driven Conservative government has all but destroyed the exceptional quality and variety of faith-based education.

There have, of course, been exceptions, but the extent of the withdrawal of the Church of England in recent years, alongside most of the other major denominations, from its engagement in the social needs of Britain is typified by one example. From the end of the Second World War, the number of children in the care of the local authority has risen sharply. The decline in family stability, an increase in the divorce rate, and the rapid rise in abortions all point to the continuing erosion of family life. In 1968 there was a total of 23,641 abortions performed in England and Wales. By 1978 this had increased to 141,558 and in 1988 to 183,798. A peak of 187,402 abortions was reached in 1998. In 2000, the most recent year for available figures, the number of abortions was 185,375 (Office for National Statistics 2001a). The number of divorces peaked in 1993 at 330,036, an increase of 23,264 from the 1990 figure of 306,772 (Office for National Statistics 2001b). Between 1991 and 2000, the number of adoptions fell from 7,170 to 4,942, leaving an ever-increasing number of older children in local authority residential care. Every single one of these numbers tells of the pain of a family in distress.

One of the main causes of these terrible statistics has been the commoditization of the individual. Since the rise of the marketing profession after the Second World War, both adults and children have increasingly been seen as units of consumption. Our value to UK plc is in the size of our wallets, and the extent to which we can be persuaded to part with our money. Advertising to children has been particularly controversial, but it works. Children see products advertised in the breaks between children's programmes, and pester their parents for them until the parent either gives in or is made to feel inadequate in refusing. The UK code of practice, set out by the Advertising Standards Authority, says that children should be able to afford the products they see in adverts – rather than rely on their parents. It adds: 'No advertising should cause children to believe that they are inferior to other children or unpopular with them if they don't buy a particular product or brand.' Unfortunately, it could be argued that this is exactly how the process works. Children feel inferior if they don't have the same things as their friends at school. Mike Jempson, director of the media ethics charity, Presswise, says: 'Serious problems are generated when children believe they control spending power: problems between children and children; between children and parents; and between parents, because they don't always agree on how to respond to children's demands' (quoted in Brown-Humes 2001).

The result of this unrelenting pressure towards commoditization has been that we collude with it. We begin to develop a world-view that sees almost every aspect of life in terms of commodities. Our homes, our possessions, even other people, are seen as valuable only when they are valuable to us, and disposable when they are not.

On 31 March 1998 it was estimated by the Government that there were around 53,300 children in local authority care, 4 per cent higher than the previous year, and 8 per cent higher than in 1994. The need for foster parents was, and remains, huge. This is an area of the nation's life where the churches could play a major part in encouraging foster parents to come forward. Most dioceses have boards for social responsibility; some, like the Diocese of Oxford, have established leading adoption agencies. Yet the funding of these boards is painfully small, their work covers a vast range of issues, and the resulting effect on the social fabric of the nation is minimal. Few congregations, if any, have active programmes to find or support foster families. Church members are not immune to the culture of commoditization, and many of us are as tied to our possessions as the rest of society. The gospel has yet to seep into the sitting room when *EastEnders* is on the television, or when the advert for the latest car leaps out at us from our favourite magazine. The idea that we might sacrifice these luxuries in order to lessen the pain of children who have no families or sitting rooms of their own hardly registers on our conscience. These are deeply spiritual issues. The problem is not simply one of vision, or rather, the lack of it. The establishment of a huge set of offices in Great Smith Street to accommodate the work of the General Synod of the Church of England has symbolized the bureaucratization of the Church's social concern; funding that could so easily have been used to establish programmes for social action that engaged with the needs of the nation has been used to produce report after report to feed debates in the General Synod, and the Church has turned its vision inward on itself to spend most of the last forty years worrying about its liturgy, its clergy and its own internal politics. Not that these reports are themselves bad, or wrong. A glance down the list of issues covered in great depth on the Church of England website under 'The Church's view on . . .' shows the deeply Christian contribution of these debates and reports to the discussion. Yet talk, without action, is less than half the answer. These debates have not impinged on the parishes in any real way, nor have they resulted in any social action of the level or significance of, say, the education movement of the late eighteenth and nineteenth century, or the great Christian social reformers that flourished during this time. The Church's role in challenging the conscience of the nation has been largely taken on by the media; it was the media, and most prominently the BBC, that took the lead in raising national awareness about the need for foster homes for the growing number of children in local authority care. And the result of this change has been felt most keenly in the parishes: those who join the local church in order to engage with the needs of their local community find, instead, that the church is almost totally disengaged. The local church sees its role almost entirely in terms of building church membership in order to engage in worship, and this becomes ultimately unsatisfying for the simple reason that Christ calls his disciples to radical change, and to the transformation of the community. He does not call us merely to fill the pews on Sunday or the house-group in midweek.

The effect of this disengagement from social needs, with its associated narrowing of the task of the Church, has been perhaps one of the biggest causes of the gap between the number of people claiming belief and the number actually participating in worship. Almost nothing can be done by the Church that has any entrepreneurial aspect, because the weight of the committee structure is simply too large, too paralysing. I remember, at the time the National Agricultural Centre launched its financial appeal for farmers, the excellent initiative of the Farming Fund, suggesting to various Church of England authorities at the very highest level that it might be helpful to have a mechanism in place to launch a national funding appeal for any future crisis. Discussion with High Street banks, the production of a template of action that included a single bank account with the provision of a call centre number, and the earmarking of staff or at least the nomination of the department to handle such an appeal, was rejected simply because the committee structures of the Church of England could not cope with the concept of planning for such high-profile engagement.

But the Church's apparent withdrawal from practical engagement with the social needs of the nation is not simply a result of a growing bureaucracy; in fact, the reverse is true. The multiplication of reports, committees, debates and officers for this, that and the other, coupled with its inability to engage creatively with national needs, is a symptom of its search for a role, not the cause of it. The first of the two great pillars on which the Church of England is built is its place as the provider, at the behest of the monarch, of spiritual care for the nation. Yet the Government, not the monarch, is now the real source of authority, and the Government has become effectively secular. While the Church of England struggles to maintain its availability to meet the needs of all of its parishioners, it has come to see those needs primarily in terms of the occasional offices. While these are a valuable point of pastoral mission, the fees set centrally fail to cover the costs, so that, for example, the Church makes a financial loss on almost every funeral service it takes.

During the past sixty years, the Church has been busy transforming itself from an institution that has the spiritual care of the nation at its heart into an organization for the maintenance of worship. That, in itself, is not necessarily a bad thing when a nation wishes to worship. But the secularization of society, which arguably reached its most visible form when the reform of the Sunday trading laws removed the one remaining sacred space from our weekly calendar, has meant that reengagement with society, not the maintenance of worship, has become the most pressing need for the Church. Establishment, in the sense that the Church exists to care for the spiritual needs of the nation, is not dead: but it is in urgent need of a new vision.

Even if the medieval concept of establishment has been weakened by official secularism, the theological principle of the Church as an agent of social transformation remains sound. A church that is only available for its participant members is an inadequate church even for them, both in its understanding of mission and in terms of transformation. It cannot be a prophetic voice, nor an agent of the Kingdom in any sense other than in the lives of its immediate participant members. But above all, it will completely ignore its associate members because it will lose any concept of relationship with the wider community, other than as a desire to use it as a lake in which to fish.

And despite the decline of a national understanding of the role of the parish, the second pillar of the Church of England, *episcope*, is probably stronger than it has been for centuries. The Church of England set out its most recent understanding of the role of its bishops in its submission to the Wakeham Commission on the reform of the House of Lords, and that submission repays careful reading. The presence of bishops in the House of Lords is one of the foundational principles of establishment, not because of the supposed privilege of which the media so often accuse the Church, nor in a representational role, but as a reflection of the responsibility placed on the Church by the monarch in his or her provision of both temporal and spiritual care for his subjects. It remains a central feature of the Church of England, and something of which the church is justifiably proud, that through the parish system its ministry is available to some of the most deprived or rural communities in the nation. Its system of support by stronger parishes for those who are less well resourced, and its regional and national interdependence, enables the bishops to provide clergy for communities where other denominations have had to withdraw.

The Wakeham submission reflects this change. The submission does not begin, as might be expected, in setting out the Church of England's understanding of itself as committed to the spiritual and pastoral care of the nation, with an exposition of the role of the established church and a defence of the position of bishops in the House of Lords; rather, it concentrates on the relationship between the bishop and his local community. It is probably true that there is no other single institution that has such a comprehensive and local knowledge of its constituents, and the role of the bishop in knowing his people means that he probably reflects the most comprehensive understanding of all. But this 'knowing' is not the cause of establishment; it is a result of it. Unique to the English constitution is the fact that the monarch has both spiritual and temporal care of his or her subjects. That spiritual care has been exercised by the Church of England is not so much a privilege (though in one sense it is), but a heavy responsibility that has been supported and financed almost exclusively by our participant members. It is something of which we can be justifiably proud. The fundamental theological principal that underlies the concept of Anglican *episcope* is simply this: 'Bear ye one another's burdens, and so fulfil the law of Christ' (Galatians 6.2 RSV). Christian congregations and communities do not, and cannot, exist by themselves or for themselves; we exist with and for each other in order to serve the purposes of God. The development of a common ministry and a way of allowing the stronger parish to support the weaker parish is central to the concept. And at a regional and national level, the mechanism whereby a stronger diocese can support a weaker one is being developed, albeit out of recent necessity, to a new level.

However, this interdependence has yet to deliver a ministry that fully reflects the opportunities presented by a society where association, rather than participation, is one of the key forms of membership. The parish, and parish ministry focused on participative membership, is still seen by most as the area of mission that has to be protected at all costs from the effects of current financial pressure. Participative membership is crucial to the mission of the Church, but only when it works to support and develop the discipleship of those who belong by association. We are moving to a new and different culture, where income will need to be earned rather than given, and partnerships, associations and contracts will increasingly play a part in an entrepreneurial church.

Principles for a Transforming Church

In order to develop a vision for the Church's ministry and mission that meets the needs of both our participant and our associative members, it might be helpful to develop some principles, and then see how those principles can be applied to the various kinds of Christian communities that make up the diversity of the Church. These principles might include the following:

- Rooted in a radical gospel.
- Based on relationships, not duty or geography.
- Meeting the needs of the nation.
- Responsive to the culture of the nation.
- Operating a centre set theology.
- Developing networks and residence.
- Restoring the place of the family.

Rooted in a Radical Gospel

The first principle of a transforming church is that it lives out a radical gospel. Jesus didn't suffer death on a cross merely to turn us into good churchgoers, no matter how charismatic, holy, disciplined, wise or compassionate our churchgoing might make us. His life, death and resurrection is a world-transforming event. His motto could well be 'I came not to bring peace, but a sword.' Even to begin to live the gospel is to be transformed in our attitudes, our lifestyle and our world-view. Our politics of exclusion, punishment and revenge will be challenged by the values of repentance, forgiveness and restoration. Our love of money, the *philoguria* that Jesus consistently calls us to renounce, will be replaced by compassion and unconditional giving. Safety will be replaced by risk. And above all, certainty will be replaced by exploration and openness to others. The Church, if it is to speak to and hold on to even its current members, let alone its potential members, will have to take seriously the demands of gospel living. And this means that God cannot remain an idea, a Christian philosophy, a way simply of making sense of the world; we have to allow him to become the *dunamis*, the dynamite or power who drives us forward, who brings both life and death, but above all, who creates transformation. The model of a church that meets together once a week for an hour's worship, that moves home because of work commitments rather than gospel imperatives, that worries about its mortgages, its telephone bills, the size of its cars or the state of its gardens – this model of church will have to give birth to other, more radical expressions of the gospel, if it is to have any hope of transforming society.

The call of the gospel is rarely to destroy, but usually to create new things. It would be a mistake to think that the traditional model of the Church is of no value, something to be put behind us, to be ignored in order to reach out to the new. Much of the language of the 'emerging church' that has become fashionable recently among a number of Evangelical Christians makes the mistake of devaluing the traditional, that which has nurtured us and brought us to where we are. The Johannine parable of the vine should make that clear. 'I am the vine,' says Jesus, 'and you are the branches' (John 15.5 RSV). I often compare the structures of the Church of England to the trunk of the vine: solid, inflexible, unexciting, and painful to knock your head against. But it supports a huge amount of growth, and provides the potential for new dynamism. So a church that lives out a radical gospel will not be stagnant, nor will it destroy what is already good and stable. Rather, it will constantly be giving birth to new forms of church membership, new expressions of gospel living, new approaches to social needs or the community's suffering. The traditional forms of church will be supportive of these new ventures, and the challenge of the new will help the traditional church regroup so that it can support them. Where the older structures make that difficult, they will be gently changed to enable the new birth to happen. Occasionally, there will be a revolutionary approach, but mostly, it will happen in an evolutionary way. Often, as with most forms of evolution and nearly all forms of spiritual growth, it will be impossible to tell from the confusion and complexity of the present precisely where the Spirit is leading us for the future. But the challenge will be to take – or even to embrace – the risks that enable the gospel to be lived afresh in each new generation.

Radical is Relative

The problem, of course, is that radicality is a relative concept. What is radical for someone only beginning to consider the claims of Christ can be the nursery slopes of the pilgrimage for others. And it is not merely a linear progression; the process of allowing different expressions of Christian discipleship is itself a radical departure from the present. If you wish to be a Christian today, you really only have two choices. The first is to join a traditional Christian congregation, usually worshipping together on a Sunday, with possible house-group meetings during the week. It is geographically fixed, when you might be spending your life on the move; it is available at one, possibly two fixed times in the week, when you might need it at other times and be totally unavailable because of family or work commitments at its main meeting times. And it will almost certainly be focused on worship, when you might have a burning call to engage with homelessness, or the environment, or some other expression of Christian discipleship. The second option is to join one of the few Christian communities, most of which are also geographically based, often enclosed orders that require lifelong commitment. Neither is necessarily the most effective option for today's culture.

Based on Relationships, not Duty or Geography

The second principle of a transforming church is that it is based on relationships, not on duty or geography. In his book on systemic thinking, *The Fifth Discipline*, Peter Senge describes the function of 'mental models'. 'Mental models', he says, 'are conceptual structures in the mind that drive cognitive processes of understanding. They influence people's actions because they mould people's appreciation of what they see.' The issue with mental models, Senge says, 'is not whether they are right or wrong, but whether they discharge routines in a person's life without them knowing' (quoted in Flood, 1999: 27). I would add that one of the functions of a mental model is to help create cohesion between individuals within a system; as an unconscious process, the mental map is powerful not simply because it helps an individual with the processes of living, but because it is a shared map that helps to create a shared understanding.

For the average church member today, the unconscious mental map that discharges his or her expectations of routine is that 'the Church' is a congregation gathered in a special building on Sundays, with the focus on worship. Furthermore, that worship will not be strongly participatory; it will usually be led by a professional, with specialist musicians, and with the congregation often only nominally participative. It is a mental model that is almost universally shared, because it is almost universally true. But the essential question is whether this understanding of the Church is fundamental to its nature, something that exists because that is what the gospel requires of the Church, or because we have inherited a developed mental map of 'the Church' that drives us to discharge the function of 'the Church' in this way. The difficulty for most of us is that tearing up the map is a frightening option. Even the suggestion that the map might be out of date, in need of redrawing, separates us from those who simply assume that the Church can only be drawn that way. And so we are driven by a combination of our unconscious mental mapping and fear of the unknown to continue with something that either does not fit our needs, or that we have no energy for. Duty takes over. We feel that in order to be a Christian, we 'ought' to go to church each Sunday, and that if we don't we are somehow failing in our Christian faith. Of course, we don't test this feeling with the question 'Can we be members of a Church that is not based on Sunday worship?', because it is not a question that easily fits our mental map. And the stronger our investment in maintaining the presence of the Church, the stranger such questions will sound to our inner ear.

But we need to learn to listen to our feelings. The sense that we 'ought' to go on doing things in any particular way, or that we 'ought' to organize the Church in a particular way, even though we have little energy for it, is one of the biggest killers of spirituality that I know. There is a proper place for duty, for obedience and discipline, but there is a real difference between the discipline of facing uncomfortable truths or difficult issues, and the mind-numbing feeling that we have to go on doing things in a particular way, that they 'ought' to be done that way, even though we have little or no energy to go on doing them. That feeling is one of the clearest indications that our mental model has got out of date, that there is a growing gap between the call of the Spirit and the worn-out paths of our mental map.

Much of the problem is caused because a large part of the life of the Church is based on duty and structures rather than on relationships and spontaneity. Yet relationships are much more fluid, much more dynamic, much more capable of responding to the needs of those engaging in them; and a Church based on relationships rather than duty is much more capable of responding to the prompting of the Spirit. For example, a group of us might have a great deal of energy to buy and repair a house in order to contribute to the needs of the single homeless. But if, having done it, we felt we had to do one a year for the rest of our lives, the project would lose its energy and become an 'ought'. The dynamism would go out of it, and we would begin to put structures in place to compensate for our loss of energy. We would tend to rely more and more on those structures to maintain the task, while our real energy was directed elsewhere.

So much of our church life is spent in servicing the structures we have put in place to compensate for our lack of energy (or simply for our boredom) that we tend to forget that the early Church was a dynamic, responsive community based on a complex set of relationships between God, the early evangelists, and their fluid and complex communities. Those communities were as varied in their beliefs as they were in their practices. The earlier New Testament letters show the fluidity and dynamism of the Church. There is little evidence there of structures or the dreaded 'ought' factor; and in one of the few places where it clearly emerges, in the letter to the Hebrews, it is condemned (see for example Hebrews 3.7–15).

The moment one begins to think about the advantages of a relationship-based church over the static structures that occupy our present mental map, they multiply considerably. For example, the potential for a non-geographically based church, one that supports its network of relationships through the Internet, for example, becomes a possibility. The option of moving from Sunday worship to a pattern of worship that meets the needs of the community is opened up. Above all, fluidity and the possibility to respond more effectively to the changing needs of the community, as well as to the prompting of the Holy Spirit, is enhanced.

What then do I mean by a relationship-based church? Simply one that values more highly the quality of relationships between its members, both associate and participative, and between those members and the God who calls them into discipleship, than it values the structures or 'mental maps' that its members have inherited. A relationship-based church deals with issues of repentance, forgiveness, calling and the deployment of gifts through a growing process of discussion and development. It focuses on the health of its members, rather than the survival of the structures. It can live happily with the concept of associative membership, because there are no boundaries to set associate members apart from participants. The edges become fuzzy, and open to relationships with people who do not hold the same kind of faith. If there is a conflict between the traditional or inherited structures, and the ability of the Church to create deep and enriching relationships between its members or between individual members and God, then it is the structures that change rather than the members. Put simply, it seems so obvious. Sadly, the strength of our unconscious 'mental map' of how 'church' should be done often makes the risk of doing things differently seem so frightening that launching into the unknown is rejected in order to cling to the traditional processes.

One objection that is raised in the Church of England to moving fully to a relationship-based model is that of public worship: if we are to provide worship for the whole community which is to be both open and accessible, how can we move from the traditional pattern? And what about canon law? The answer is reasonably simple. A group of people can choose to provide public worship in order to create the opportunity of new relationships. After all, isn't that what already happens? Or is it another case of structures doing for us what we have lost the will to do for ourselves?

Meeting the Needs of the Nation

Engaging the faith of those who belong by association is not going to be achieved by inviting them to participate in church structures or worship. It can, however, be done by listening to their needs, and by responding appropriately. One of the most powerful stories in the Gospels is the story of the blind man that Jesus meets begging on the road to Jericho (Luke 18.35–43 RSV). The man calls out to him: 'Jesus, son of David, have mercy on me.' Here was someone who was denied participation in normal everyday social life because of a physical need. Jesus could well have simply presumed that he knew what the man needed. Instead, he invites a response: 'What do you want me to do for you?'. The response is a practical one: 'Sir, I want my sight.' The question presupposes power, both in the asking: 'What do you want me to do for you?', and in the response: 'Sir, I want my sight.' The fact that Jesus responds by evoking the man's need is a clear lesson. It would be interesting to ask the same question of those who criticize the Church, or who stand apart from membership. But the question requires that we listen to the answer, and it may not be very comfortable.

If this simple story is not enough to convince us that one of the primary tasks of the Church is to evoke and meet the needs of our neighbour, then the story of the Good Samaritan must be. Here, the question 'Who is my neighbour?', asked by a lawyer in order to explore the limit of our responsibility under God, is answered more profoundly. My neighbour is whoever needs my help at this moment. So fulfilling the command to 'Love God, and love my neighbour as myself' simply means responding to others' needs when we become aware of them. That agenda should provide the Church with a task sufficient to keep it focused!

At the heart of a transforming church is the desire to meet the needs, not only of our members, but also of the community in which we are set. The question is similar: 'Who is my neighbour?' If we are not engaged with the needs of the community around us, then we will not satisfy the spiritual longings of those who are our members, and will not engage with those who belong by association. It is an interesting test. Whenever a church or a Christian leader decides to engage in a new area of ministry, there are usually people who come from right outside the church – people who are associate members, whose believing is their belonging – who step forward to help.

Such engagement may certainly be costly, particularly when the needs of the poor or the disadvantaged clash with the official policies of the local community. In the early 1980s, I was working as a parish priest in east Winchester. Winchester was not known for its poverty; in fact, on most scales of measurement it was at that time one of the wealthiest areas of the country. Yet, as is often the case with areas of wealth, the statistics masked small – and not so small – areas of considerable deprivation. One of the problems we faced, created in no small part by the policies of a government whose leader openly stated that she didn't believe there was any such thing as society, was that of young, single homeless people. Young people, because of abuse at home, or because they were unable to make the transition from home to independence, were living rough on the streets. There was an advice centre, but the city council, Conservative to the core and presumably sharing the belief of their leader, withdrew its funding. Now one of the glories of Winchester, despite the best efforts of the planning authority to surround it with concrete monstrosities, is its cathedral. The cathedral draws thousands of tourists, and is set in a beautiful oasis of green grass right in the centre of the city. And the dean, who in his life and ministry had faced far tougher authorities than Winchester City Council, was not happy with this decision. So he let it be known that unless the council restored the funding, he would allow a Portacabin or three on to the cathedral green, with a very large sign proclaiming it the Winchester Homeless Advice Centre. It was, apparently, enough to embarrass the council into action.

This may be an apocryphal story – it was certainly doing the rounds in Winchester at the time that the council gave money to a rival homelessness project – but from personal experience I can attest to the appointment at about the same time, by the city council, of a housing welfare officer who visited homes on my rundown council estate and did everything he could to frighten the residents so as to prevent the council from having to find housing for the homeless that they were supposedly helping. One house, designated as so-called 'short-term emergency accommodation', had been home to one family for seven years. They had no hot water, the plaster was falling from the walls, and the elderly father had a chronic illness made worse by the damp and the cold. There wasn't even an electric point upstairs from which water could be heated. This was not inner-city Liverpool, or deprived Manchester; it was wealthy Winchester. And challenging the situation led to real pain for the Church.

Such small-scale challenges are by no means unique; stories such as these can be repeated in most churches and in most situations across the country. But there are things that cannot be done effectively by individual churches and congregations; they need either regional or national action. Such action in the past, for example in the provision of schools or the abolition of child labour, was done on a national basis. Future needs, such as the possibility of working with the large number of children in local authority care, can also best be done from a national, or at least a regional, base. The Church, if it is to regain any kind of credibility, needs to change its structures so that it can take that regional or national action. It cannot rely on the various parachurch organizations to do its work for it.

Responsive to the Culture of the Nation

The next principle for a transforming church is that it should be responsive to the changing culture of the nation. This is what incarnation is about – making the eternal nature of God present, visible and relevant in each new generation. And it is here that there is the greatest contrast between the medieval parish system and today's society. As we have already seen in previous chapters, there are at least four major differences between our culture and the culture for which the parish system was devised. Very broadly, and at the risk of making sweeping generalizations, they are mobility and membership, nearly universal education, disintermediation, and communication.

The inability of the Church to adapt its structures to meet the needs of a changing culture has had a major effect in creating membership by association. Nearly all of the assumptions on which parish ministry is based are assumptions about the local stability of the population. Membership of the Church of England is a difficult legal question, because the determination of membership has evolved over many hundreds of years, and with a number of different criteria. Baptism, confirmation, the reception of Holy Communion once a year, and membership of the electoral roll each constitute an independent criterion for saying 'I belong'. One classic example of this local thinking is the baptism register. Baptism is the most universal recognition of membership of the Church. When you are baptized in an Anglican church (or in any other Trinitarian church for that matter) you are made a member of the universal Christian Church. Yet when an infant is brought for baptism in the Church of England, his or her name is recorded in a book kept in the safe of the parish church. There is no central register of the baptized, simply because the assumptions about membership are based on the parish church. So if, as is most likely today, the family move away from the parish in the early years of the child's life, there is no way of keeping in contact with the family. It is rare for a parish priest to refer a family onwards to their new parish. And it is even rarer for that family to make contact with the parish church in their new locality to register the fact that the church has made a commitment to nurture the faith of the child and bring him or her to confirmation.

The electoral roll, which is the register of those who have committed themselves to membership of the Church, is also a locally based register. It is the property of the parochial church council, a public document that cannot legally be used by the diocese or by any other body in order to communicate with the members of the Church. Neither is the register of those who have been confirmed, who have chosen to express the fullest statement of membership of the Church of England, kept centrally. Names are submitted to the bishop, but not contact details, and this data is not used for any other purpose than the recording of names, and producing annual confirmation numbers. The overall effect of all of this is that the Church of England simply does not have any regional or central register of its members. We simply don't know at any regional level who we have baptized, where our confirmed members live, or who belongs to our churches. And why should we? After all, the parish system is based on the assumptions that people live in the same community for life, and that there is no need to do anything more than encourage them to come to worship. The duty of the curate, clearly set out in the Book of Common Prayer, is to chase up those infants who have not been baptized, to teach children the catechism, and to encourage parents to bring their baptized children for confirmation when they are old enough. It was a good system for a community where the population was manageable, where mobility was limited, and where the concept of Christendom, albeit in a modified form, still operated. But for today's Church, it is not only inappropriate and unmanageable; the lack of any central or even regional organization of membership makes the Christian education of baptized children, or the exercising of our declared responsibility for bringing up those we have baptized in the faith of the Church, almost impossible if the family move or lose contact with their baptizing church. The outcome is a large number of children who have been baptized, but whose faith has never been educated. These children have grown into adults and had children of their own and have brought them for baptism because they have a sense of belonging. But because they themselves have never been challenged about their faith, or taught any modern equivalent of a catechism, or brought to confirmation, their sense of belonging is associative, rather than participative. Our abrogation of responsibility to maintain contact with those we have baptized has been a direct contributing factor to the gap between those who believe and those who belong.

The Church of England, alongside other churches, is not the only organization to suffer from dispersed membership. The Conservative Party, whose membership is formed through a federation of local associations, has found it equally difficult to manage the education or development of its membership base. By contrast, the Labour Party, with its more recent foundation and history, has a centralized membership structure and has found it much easier to recruit new members, as well as make appeals for funding or discuss constitutional change.

The need for centralized membership is a direct response to the cultural change from membership based on local participation to membership based on national association: the effect of disintermediation, which seeks direct contact and communication with the source, or the centre, wherever that is perceived to be. Communication with participant members, though difficult in a dispersed membership organization, is not impossible. But communication with associate members is another matter. Few local branches have the level of resources or organization to mount major communication initiatives. The idea of a direct mail shot might be feasible for a regional headquarters or a diocese; it becomes completely impossible to manage through a variety of differing local branches or parishes.

Open All Hours

One of the surprises of the 1990s was the revival of the cinema. In the 1980s, cinema-going in this country was in decline. The home video, the black box that could record films off the air and replay them in your own sitting room, coupled with the 'one size fits all' approach of film distributors, hit the film industry hard. Broadcasting was seen as the new form of cinema, and the birth of the satellite television industry, which led to the rapid growth of new television channels, all but signalled the end of the cinema. But a remarkable change was about to take place. The cinema fought back.

What happened was that film distributors recognized that the experience of a single 'double bill' showing in the one-screen, scruffy and frankly slightly smelly building that had been the traditional experience of cinema-going could be turned around. The aim was to create a whole new experience of cinema-going. Brand-new buildings were erected, containing not one screen, but many. Often up to six or seven small auditoria were built, each with a much more intimate feel, and with new, clean furniture. Sound systems were improved. And the public loved it. Going to the cinema was no longer a matter of queueing outside in the rain for a single choice of film, and watching it in a half-empty cavern of a building that smelled of last year's sweat. There was light. There was intimacy. And above all, there was choice. The result was that cinema-going has grown exponentially since the introduction of the multiplex. Costs were driven down, because far more people could see far more films in a single building; staffing and equipment costs were considerably lower. And with the reduction in staffing costs came economies of scale in advertising, in heating and lighting, and in the provision of the cinema-goer's favourite snack, popcorn. Alongside these multiplex cinemas were built fast-food shops, pubs, restaurants, so that going to the cinema became a whole evening's experience. No more badly made trailers with their tacky maps showing the 'Tandoori restaurant' one hundred yards up the street, across the square and behind Marks and Spencer. You came out of the cinema, and your choice of food or drink was a mere step or two away – often under cover so you didn't even have to remember the umbrella.

Now I'm not for a moment suggesting that we need to have multiplex churches, with small chapels for different denominational services, surrounded by fast-food bars. But the principles that led to the renewal of cinema-going can be applied to a relationship-based church. The four major principles are: (1) the relative mobility of the population and its willingness to use that mobility to engage in leisure activities, (2) the use of economies of scale that allow a richer variety of experience, (3) the recognition that people want to watch a film when they choose, rather than when the cinema chooses to show it, and (4) the sense of intimacy created by much smaller, fuller, cleaner and more modern auditoria compared to the single, cavernous and often more than half-empty old theatre-style buildings. Rather than holding on to a large number of small, single-purpose church buildings, it would be perfectly possible in centres of high population for the Church to develop complex centres where the full range of Christian ministry would be available. Simply by using economies of scale, it would be easier, not more difficult, for these centres to service the communities in their area.

And so the next principle of a transforming and transformed church is that it can be responsive to the culture in which it is set by using economies of scale to increase its availability. Anthony Russell, the former area bishop of Dorchester, has begun to experiment with what he calls 'major benefices', an idea which is based on the Augustinian model of a regional centre with a mixed team of lay and ordained members serving the small parishes around it.

Operating a Centre Set Theology

A vision for a Church that engages with the nation must include within itself a vision for dialogue and exploration with the various expressions of spirituality of the nation. The idea of centre set theology, as opposed to the closed set mentality that infects so much of our current church-going, was fully discussed in Chapter 4. Suffice it to say here that engagement with many of the newer forms of spirituality can only happen when the local Christian community operates in an open or centre set way. Excluding all those with whom you disagree is not only an unhealthy way to behave as a community; it is also a very poor model for engaging with the large number of people who belong by association, because you are rarely able to engage in dialogue with those who wish to explore the transcendent with you, but who come from a very different starting point.

So the next principle for constructing a church that is able to engage with, and transform, the society in which it is set is that it must operate a centre set model of participation. Such a way of working is by no means easy, and autocratic clergy and ministers, who wish to limit (in the name of pastoring, of course) the spiritual experiences of their congregations to what they approve, will find it almost impossible. But it has to be done. We need to train clergy and lay leaders to operate in this way, without either losing their passion for Christianity, or giving in to those who wish to exclude all other forms of spiritual expression. The days of Saint Boniface, who converted Germany by cutting down the sacred oak of Wotan and demonstrating that he didn't get roasted for his impertinence by an angry God, are long past. As John Finney has clearly shown, conversion is a process that takes years, not weeks or months, and is best engaged in by dialogue and non-judgemental friendship (Finney 1992).

Networks and Residence – or 'An Hour Is Not Enough'

The next principle for a transformed church is that an hour once a week on a Sunday is not enough to enable the kind of transformation of life that a radical gospel requires. Even a collection of hours, spent week after week on hard pews, is not enough. In order to engage in real relationships, we need real communities. We need to recreate the kind of religious communities that converted England in the Dark Ages, but in a form that can be most accessible to people today. There are a number of factors that drive us towards the need for residential communities – ashrams by another name. Community only really becomes genuine when you have to learn, usually over a number of days or weeks, to live together in a common life of prayer, study and relaxation. In the early days of the house church movement, some form of community living was often the powerhouse behind their phenomenal growth. Alongside and within the traditional parish structures, it would be perfectly possible to create residential communities that are wider, more dispersed, than the old enclosed orders.

Take, for example, a group of people operating a centre set model of spirituality, who express part of their spiritual life by living in the community house for a number of days, or weeks, a year. During their intern week, they have the support of a structured prayer life, regular study, and informal discussion with other community members. For a large part of the year, they live a 'normal' life with their families, or at work, or wherever. But for a few days they retreat to their community, spending time in prayer, quiet, study, relaxation and informal discussion. The core members of the community may well spend longer in residence – they may spend months at a time, or even longer – but there is no commitment to stay for life. Part of their Christian giving is devoted to the support of their community, and part of the work of the community is to take in a proportion of people with real needs – spiritual, emotional or physical. The members of the community, whether they are 'dispersed' or 'interns', keep in touch with one another through the Internet, which in itself is a form of open access for the maintenance of relationships.

Restoring the Place of the Family

The final principle for a transforming church is the importance of the family, or the small community that corresponds to the family, in the ritual and practice of Christian discipleship. A faith that is not lived out in the home is not a fully dynamic faith. Daily prayer, meditation and study are vital ingredients in the Christian life, and not nearly enough attention is given to these by the average local church. I have already argued at length that the primary covenant community identified in the Old Testament is the extended family; the main ritual which affirms that community under the old covenant is the Passover, celebrated by the family in the family home once a year. The new Passover, the eucharist, was transferred from the home to the place of worship fairly early in the life of the Church, but the results of this, combined with the clericalization of worship, has diminished the central role of the family and disabled one of the key areas of mission and pastoral care.

We have to find ways of restoring the centrality of the family, and of transferring some of the clericalized activities back to their proper place in the home. The teaching of our children, the development of local Christian service, the place of the agapé meal, even the celebration of the eucharist in the home with the family elder presiding – all of these are possible options once the principle of the centrality of the family, or the extended small community that substitutes for the family, is restored.

These, then, are the key principles of a transformed and transforming church that is open enough to work not only with its participant members, but also with those who choose to belong by association:

- Rooted in a radical gospel.
- Based on relationships, not duty or geography.
- Meeting the needs of the nation.
- Responsive to the culture of the nation.
- Operating a centre set theology.
- Developing networks and residence.
- Restoring the place of the family.

It will be interesting to see if, and how, these principles can be applied to the various forms of traditional or inherited Christianity, so that we can help create a church that is responsive and suited to the new opportunities around us, and that will serve both its participant and its associative members.

Chapter 7

Transforming the Parish Church

Throughout this book I have argued that the Church has two kinds of members. According to the churches themselves, those who belong by participation, who join the rotas, serve on the parochial church council (PCC), populate the pews on Sunday and take part in the house groups, make up between 12 and 14 per cent of the population. And according to the 2001 Opinion Research Business (ORB) survey, those who belong by association, who rarely attend but would claim, and claim quite strongly, to be members, make up 73 per cent of the population (Heald 2001). This gap of 59 per cent may at first sight seem far too large to be credible. And as a measure of those who belong by association to the Church of England it clearly is. But it is not an isolated figure. Survey after survey has come up with a similar gap. What it shows is that there is a huge gap – made up of nearly 60 per cent of the population – who claim some form of allegiance to Christian believing but who do not participate in any meaningful way in a local church. A relatively small proportion of the nation chooses participative membership, but a very large proportion chooses to belong by association. On any reading, the figure contains within it a sizeable proportion of people who genuinely feel that they belong to a Christian community. That sense of belonging may be specific enough to identify with a particular denomination, of which the Church of England will probably be the largest. But even if it does not, the fact remains that the Church of England, along with all the other expressions of Christian believing in this nation, will have to take the figures very seriously indeed.

So how does that peculiarly Anglican phenomenon, the parish church, respond to the demands of a changing culture in a way that can serve both its participant and its associate members? And how can it be rooted in a radical gospel, valuing relationships above structures, and engaging with the nation and the family unit in a way that can become transformational?

The parish church is unique in denominational terms because it has a given mission statement, which is to serve the Kingdom by serving all those who live within the parish borders, regardless of their religious affiliation. This task is a given which is shared with all the other parishes in the Church of England, and the Church of England is justifiably proud of its record in this area, for in spite of huge financial pressures in maintaining both its buildings and its ordained ministry, it has continued to serve both inner cities and sparsely populated rural areas where other denominations have been forced to withdraw. This commitment stems, as we have already seen, from the monarch's responsibility to care for both the spiritual and the temporal well-being of her subjects. It is exercised through the special position of its bishops. And it will continue to be a given, regardless of financial or structural issues, for as long as the Church of England continues to hold a missiology that rejects congregationalism and affirms the place of the spiritual in the life of the nation as a whole.

Yet, more and more, the parish church is in crisis. It has both a crisis of identity and a crisis of role, and has tended over the past fifty years to make that crisis worse rather than better through adopting more and more what I have called a 'closed set' mentality. The introduction of the parish communion as the main act of worship on a Sunday has tended to exclude those who are not confirmed, which is probably one of the narrowest definitions of participant membership. By doing so, the parish church has put itself into direct competition with other congregationally based churches, and has consistently measured itself against a presumed benchmark of committed participant membership. Yet it is not designed for this kind of membership. And the stress and loss of identity is compounded by changes in our culture. We live in an age of disintermediation, when people choose to bypass the local branch in order to go direct to source, and in terms of spirituality, that means that people who belong by association are increasingly disconnected from the local representation of the Church, and increasingly looking to alternative forms of spirituality that promise (and occasionally deliver) a quick spiritual fix, or a connection to the sacred that bypasses the vicar and his local congregation.

In theological terms, the critique of the parish church – the test by which it can determine its faithfulness to its task – is not that of membership, but that of the cross: the self-emptying of God, who accepts death in order to release life. Only as the parish church, as a community of local Christian disciples, allows itself to enter fully into the experience of crucifixion can it regain both its identity and its role, for it is only when local people can experience the radical transformation brought about by a small community living according to the values of the cross that they will recognize the real attraction of membership of the community of the cross. The problem is that while the Church preaches the cross, and venerates the cross at the heart of its worship, it lives a life that is at odds with the cross. It worries about money, about its institutional position, about its status. This is, in effect, a loss of vision and a loss of faith.

There is a longing in most parish churches, among both clergy and people, for a rediscovery of mission and ministry that reflects the reality of the cross, because in their hearts they know that only by living the faith of the crucified can they change. Yet there is also a paralysis that has gripped many of those who are open to change, simply because it is difficult to imagine what shape the Church might take. We have got so used to planning, and have so clearly adopted a mechanistic approach to ministry, that we want to be able to see a model of the future Church so that we can construct it ourselves. Thankfully, the cross calls us to a different process. The only way that we are going to discover the shape of the future Church is to embrace the cross, to allow ourselves to enter into crucifixion, and in the process to discover that it is we who are being remade, and that the remaking of the Church can only follow our transformation, not precede it. We will discover the shape of the future Church by engaging ourselves with the process, rather than trying to be detached builders of something that is yet to be formed.

So how can we begin to take the plunge, to become swimmers rather than spectators? And the answer is that, both from a practical and a psychological perspective, it is hard to do it on our own. We need the support and the stimulation of others who are equally motivated, but we also need to be able to step outside our own parochialism, and to embrace the wider perspective, in order to be able to recognize the best 'stepping off' point. Let me give a specific example.

As I was preparing the outline of this chapter, I happened to see an advertisement for a new vicar for a parish in a small market town. The main emphasis in the details sent to applicants for this post was on the problem of maintaining the building so that it could continue its ministry. Yet there were three other Anglican churches in the town, and they had a combined electoral roll of just over 2 per cent of the town's population. Quite apart from the huge evangelistic issues raised, there was nothing in the details about any kind of collaborative ministry, nothing that gave any hint that trying to maintain four churches with a combined electoral roll of only 2 per cent of the population might be a mistaken strategy. I came to the conclusion, admittedly from a distance, that the only way the issues of evangelization could be tackled was by a communal recognition that embracing the cross might mean a new kind of mission strategy that was not concerned with maintaining structures, but building relationships. This kind of change is simply not possible unless people meet to pray for the courage to embrace the cross. That embrace is both scary yet longed for. It is like the start of a passionate relationship, where the end is unknown but the travel is exhilarating.

Part of the difficulty in re-imagining the local parish church is that we continue to expect everyone to go to it. We cannot see that it is in the nature of the local church to act as a core group, providing resources for those who do not attend. If you look at the structure of, for example, the Greenpeace movement, you will see that the core values and beliefs are modelled and acted out by a very small group of committed members. But in modelling those values and beliefs, that small core act as a symbol to the rest of us, drawing us in to their values and beliefs, simply because we can relate to their actions. Some of those actions might appear extreme to us, but in terms of transmitting beliefs and values, they demonstrate both commitment and passion. They are news not because of a good public relations department, though that is clearly at work; they are news because they are newsworthy. They act both as symbol and reality; they model in a big way what might be possible for us in a small way. And in supporting the commitment, the passion, of those core members who climb on board the ships carrying radioactive waste, or who chain themselves to polluting oil platforms, we are ourselves changed. We take part more willingly in the recycling of our own waste, and in the smaller political actions that transform our own communities.

In exactly the same way, the local parish church needs to become a centre for local activists. But the activity that we need to model is the embracing of the cross, not the recruitment of more participant members. The size of the congregation, the core group, is almost irrelevant. What matters is the quality and depth of commitment. It is when we meet to pray for the courage to embrace transformation that we begin to be transformed. And the nature and direction of that transformation will depend almost entirely on the demands of the cross for our own community. For some, it might mean engagement in homelessness issues. For others, it might mean the development of community. Or again, it might take some form of political action. But the energy at the heart of the transformation will be the willingness to accept the personal change of lifestyle and direction that is demanded by the cross. Only by embracing the transforming nature of crucifixion can the local parish church hope to find resurrection. There is no other way; nothing that can be done from the outside can restore the identity or the role of the local church.

And, maybe surprisingly, this transformation is by far the best way that the local parish church can serve those who belong by association. Just as the activists of the Greenpeace movement have energized and engaged those who share their values and beliefs, so too can the local community of Christian activists energize and engage those who are tired of the secular materialism of our culture, but who currently fail to see in the Church a real alternative. The gospel will be seen because it will be lived, and the gospel is good news because it takes us, quite literally, out of ourselves and into engagement with God, and with the needs of those around us. It opens our eyes to other people's pain, and calls us to walk alongside them in solidarity and support.

How then can the local parish church engage in such transformation? The answer has to be through a combination of worship and preaching that takes risks, and in the meeting of small groups of people who pray for the courage to embrace change. But it can only happen if we are willing to embrace the risk of failure, because that is how crucifixion can seem to those outside the Church. For the Roman authorities, the death of Jesus was simply the end of a problem. For the friends of Jesus, his death appeared to be the ultimate failure of their hopes. Yet through the eyes of faith, his death was not merely the herald of new life, it was the means to new life.

In many churches that I visit, I am struck by the number of people who continue to do things for which they have little or no energy, simply because that is the way things 'ought' to be done. They go on doing things because this is simply how they have always been done. To risk change is to risk alienation or failure. The admission of this loss of energy, the loss of belief in the system, is perhaps the most important starting point. If we are willing to admit that the Church has lost its appeal, lost its attraction, then we might be taking the first tentative step towards embracing the cross. How often have we heard about those who have given up their faith, who have left the Church, and who say afterwards: 'The funny thing is, I didn't really miss it.' This is the real tragedy, and it is one for which we bear responsibility if we too feel the need to change, but refuse to take the risk of confessing that need.

The next step, once this need for change is admitted, is to begin the process of re-imagining our own discipleship. We might wish to spend time in retreat, or we might spend time with a few people who share our longing, to learn from the gospels about risk-taking. But unlike the house group that continually discusses the gospel, we need to begin to live it. That is the painful decision, because it will cost us, in the first place, our security, and ultimately our lives. But this is always how renewal begins – not by expecting the Holy Spirit to give us the missing power, but by our being willing to embrace the possible pain and cost of the cross. It was by embracing the risk and pain of rejection that the great reformers like the

Earl of Shaftesbury were able to take others with them. It was by embracing the risk of rejection, and the huge personal cost of possible compensation, that those who opposed slavery were able to make progress. And it will only be by taking the risk of losing status, wealth and security that we can begin the transformation of our local church.

I have said before that Jesus didn't die a painful death on a cross merely to turn us into good churchgoers. He died to change us, and through us, to change the communities and groups in which we live. To change implies movement, but that movement does not have to be uniform, nor all in one direction. One of the features of a local church in the process of transformation will be that it becomes more chaotic, more open to creative tensions and new directions. There may be a small group of members who wish to explore community living. They will share their vision with the Church, and gain its support. Again, there may be those who wish to take smaller steps, to sit with the housebound, or to visit the local prison or hospital. Some may wish to meet early, before work, for prayer or Bible study. Others may have a vision for youth work, or children's work. The patterns of transformation will almost certainly be uneven. But the Church will be there to provide support for all of these initiatives. It will not be a controlling organization, but a liberating community. We need to remember that it was the overshadowing of chaos by the Spirit of God that produced the dynamic for creation.

One of the most interesting aspects of this kind of transformation is the change in the centrality of worship. We have assumed, because (as we have seen previously) we have inherited a pattern of the Church that dates back to the monastic communities of the early Middle Ages, that worship has to be at the heart of our church life. But we have developed this concept so that worship is not simply the centre of our church life, but its sole activity. So heavily does this centrality of organized worship dominate our mental map that it is hard to see how it could be otherwise. After all, isn't that what 'the Church' is for? To provide services of worship that the whole community can attend? And the answer, surprisingly, is 'maybe not'. Maybe discipleship, rather than worship, should be at the core of our church life. And discipleship can embrace a whole world of activities, aspirations and values that ritual worship, by itself, cannot. A church may meet together just as faithfully to engage in serving the homeless, or reaching out to the poor, as it can to worship. In fact, it may discover that by taking the service of the poor, or the care of the homeless, as its central activity, its worship becomes transformed, and its doors become more open to those who long to participate but who at the moment cannot see the point.

Public Worship and Personal Discipleship

This aspiration, felt by many in the Church, leads to one of the most difficult tensions, particularly for the Anglican Church: the tension between personal discipleship and public worship. The parish church has to provide a centre for public worship – it has to be, and to remain, open and available to all those who live within its parish boundaries. It has to be available for those who wish to come to pray, to reflect, or to take time out with God. And it needs to remain local, and to be rooted in the aspirations, frustrations and social dynamics of its own community. In order to resolve this tension between personal discipleship and public worship, its focus must move from its own agenda to the agenda of those amongst whom it lives. Although this is only the first step, it can sometimes be the hardest step to take, because it requires a fundamental change of perspective. It requires church members to see their engagement with their world not as something to be left behind at the church door, but as the substance of their prayers, their house-group discussions, their preaching, their church management, and above all their time. It is this public focus, above all else, that equips the local parish church to become a resource for those who belong by association as well as participation.

The change can develop from many beginnings. One might be a setting aside of the normal 'housekeeping' agenda of the PCC in favour of discovering a local agenda that resonates with the community (such as homelessness, or the isolated elderly, or traffic problems). I remember when our church discussed the issue of Sunday trading. It could well have been one of those desultory half-discussions, when those present simply talked around the subject for fifteen minutes, with an inconclusive finish. But we were concerned to make a statement that would enable church members to affirm a position, and that would inform the local discussions that were taking place over local shopping hours. So we decided to hold an open meeting. Members of the church were invited to discuss a preliminary position paper, and the meeting was widely advertised. Anyone who wished could have a copy of the preliminary paper (today, it would have been available on the church website, for downloading by anyone who needed it, but at that time it was produced in hard copy).

The result of this twin action of producing a preliminary paper and advertising a meeting on an issue that was engaging a considerable section of the community meant that we attracted a far wider audience than we had expected. Several teachers turned up, as did at least two local councillors. One or two shopkeepers came. Many of them were people who we would only see occasionally, if ever, on a Sunday. But they all claimed some kind of allegiance to the Christian Church, and a number were clearly associate, rather than participative, members. We discussed, in considerable depth, the issues raised by the preliminary paper, and came to a number of conclusions. These were duly set out in a second paper, and circulated to all who were at the meeting. They were invited to send their considered response to a coordinator, who would produce a final position paper. This was then presented to an open meeting of the whole church on a weekday evening. The result was that the second meeting was attended by a large number of people who rarely, if ever, worshipped with us on a Sunday. But more than this, they had created a number of bridges into their own networks. One of the councillors presented our concluding paper at a meeting of the local town council; another used it in school. It became our church's position on Sunday trading, and was widely respected locally, even if it was perhaps ignored by the national trading chains like Tesco, who always do what they want regardless of the local community. As such, it became almost a subversive action. Many churches will have similar stories to tell.

It is often when the Church crosses the traditional boundaries it has created to protect itself, or has allowed to be created by others in order to authenticate distance, that it grows. Another example of this boundary crossing comes from my experience of working with the pagan community in the UK. A few years ago, sitting at my desk in Oxford's Diocesan Church House, I had a telephone call from the national church offices. There is an ancient stone circle called the Rollright Stones in a small rural parish to the west of the diocese. The farmer who owned the stones was intending to sell them, and had invited groups to bid. One of these groups was a local group of pagans. The pagans were concerned that the stones should not be 'Disneyfied' by an entrepreneurial group, or 'officialized' by the National Trust. They had sought, and obtained, promises of funding from a number of famous individuals, including (allegedly) the creator of the Discworld books, Terry Pratchett. A vicar of one of the local parishes had objected publicly to this bid, imagining all sorts of dark occult practices taking place around the stones. The local row had escalated into the national newspapers along the lines of 'Archbishop versus Terry Pratchett', and as Director of Communications for the diocese, I was asked to intervene. Not getting very far with the local vicar, I decided to speak with the pagan group, and was warmly welcomed. They too were worrying about the escalation of the row, and I was invited to share the Christian position on the local radio station in dialogue with one of the leading pagans, Karin Atwood. The result of this intervention was an invitation to take part in further Christian–

pagan dialogue, and from there the relationships have developed to the point where quiet, sensitive and open dialogue is regularly taking place between a small group of Christians and pagans. For the first time this year I attended the Pagan Federation's annual conference. It was quietly satisfying to go in my dog collar, to be greeted warmly at the entrance by one of the country's well-known witches, and to receive a round of applause from the assembly of pagans for my work with the Rollright Stones group.

Such crossing of boundaries is risky; it is easily misunderstood by those on both sides of the divide, and just as easily undone by a refusal to embrace the cross. But the risk is based on sound theology: first, on the theology of incarnation itself, but also on the cross and the resurrection. For only by taking risks in crossing such boundaries can the Church open up new avenues for dialogue and mission. Sometimes these will be corporate ventures, led by a decision of the PCC or a sub-group of it. Sometimes they will be led by house-groups, or by individuals. They might happen in a planned fashion, like the discussion on Sunday trading, or as a result of following an opportunity, as with the Rollright Stones group. But they can, and should, inform the prayers of the local church, either publicly (as with the Sunday trading issues) or privately (as with the Rollright Stones group). The parish church becomes the supporting base for individuals or groups called to cross boundaries. It should, of course, exercise pastoral oversight and judgement in assessing the risks involved, but it should never be afraid of taking those risks that it believes will create new opportunities for dialogue, service and exploration.

One of the most pressing of needs is for the local church to embrace the aspirations and culture of the young people amongst whom it lives. Again, it cannot do this remotely, by adults assuming to speak for young people. It has to find ways of connecting with the culture of the young, and engaging them in dialogue. Such dialogue may be practical, rather than verbal. The development of a park for skateboarders, or the provision of space for meeting, are simple examples of first-step activities. Local church members will have their own vision, no doubt led by their own experience of young people in their community. But such engagement should be forged and developed by supporting the aspirations of young people, not by assuming to speak or act on their behalf. It is remarkably risky to allow young people to explore their spirituality without boundaries, but it is a risk well worth taking; it is an even greater risk to alienate them and prevent such exploration within the context of the local church.

The parish church can be instrumental in many local initiatives. But it needs to be able to hold these in tension with its public worship so that it engages through its preaching, its prayers and its pastoral care with the whole range of its community. Those who come to church, perhaps for the first time, on a Sunday morning need to see not only the piety of its members, but also their engagement with local issues. Those who come to find the warmth of human friendship need to see that this is available not only at coffee after the service, but in the local school, or at the church's favourite pub, or with coffee in the homes of its members. Love becomes sacrificial because it gives itself to those who need it.

Such engagement with the local community will flow over into the experience of those who bring their children for baptism, those who come to seek confirmation, those who come to be married, and those whose families come following bereavement. It will flow into the civic services and symbolic rituals that link church and community. It will create all kinds of bridges between the sacred mystery that we worship at the heart of the universe and the community in which we live. The key task will be to change the focus of the local church from its own processes, from its focus on supporting those who come as participant members, to a focus on the needs and aspirations of the local community. Such a change in focus will allow us to celebrate the faith and Christian commitment of those who do not currently attend worship. It will enable us to become a centre set church, exploring with confidence the dynamics of a life and faith based on the cross, rather than a protective closed set community that is more concerned with its own survival than with the world for which Christ died.

Chapter 8

Cathedrals as Centres of Association

Cathedrals are the parts of the Church most likely to be able to relate to, and work with, those who belong by association. They are ultimately non-participative, deliberately so in most cases. Until fairly recently, those who were engaged with cathedral mission had often been heard to comment privately on the uncertainty they felt about the role of the cathedral in the mission of the Church. The material needs of these huge buildings, often Grade 1-star listed, consume enormous amounts of energy, and raising the several thousand pounds a day needed to maintain and run them is not easy. Many of them have wonderful musical foundations – the 'living art' of choirs and musicians that raise choral music from 'mere' music to an art form that is itself a form of spirituality. Many have world-heritage-class art and artefacts in addition to their buildings, all of which require careful and expensive conservation, display and security.

So until the fairly recent past, cathedrals have tended to see themselves as guardians of the Church's heritage, centres of worship for the diocese and the diocesan bishop, and major tourist attractions. Yet the current popularity of cathedral worship and witness, particularly after a whole series of national and international difficulties such as rail crashes, the death of Princess Diana, and terrorist attacks in the United States, together with the consequent growth of their attendance figures in direct contrast to the decline in parish church attendance, has focused the Church's attention on its cathedrals in a way probably unheard of since the Middle Ages. And there is good reason for this. The focus of the parish church as the centre of participant membership has not served those who belong by association. It has reinforced, rather than demolished, the difficulties of access that the Church has placed in the way of those who belong by association, or who do not yet belong at all. The parish church has increasingly demanded commitment in regular worship through participation in rotas and house-groups, and in demanding doctrinal understanding of a high level when it comes, in particular, to baptisms, weddings and sometimes even funerals. It has not done what its name suggests, which is to make Christian faith and ritual available to the parish, to those who belong by association, those who rarely come, and those who wish to have access to the mystery of God without the requirement of commitment to the domestic life of the Church.

Cathedrals, on the other hand, have almost everything going for them in today's culture. Their buildings speak of ancient wisdom, which is highly appealing in a fast-moving and transient culture. In a survey of men in their thirties who do not attend church, undertaken by St Peter's Church, High Wycombe, the value of ancient buildings in giving a sense of solidity to the Christian gospel was surprisingly strong. The myth that ancient buildings alienate those who belong by association, and that we should concentrate on a 'buildingless' church, is just that – a myth.

The concept of pilgrimage is also alive and flourishing – making a spiritual journey to discover a spiritual truth often takes people not to the local church (though they might, if they persevered, discover that the local church is just as capable of providing spiritual awakening, through encounter with local people who are themselves following a spiritual path), but to the cathedral. Drawn by the size, the architecture, sometimes the simple openness of its worship, the cathedral acts as a magnet to hundreds of thousands of people who visit it, both as a cultural experience and as a spiritual pilgrimage. Increasingly, cathedrals are recognizing that the development of pilgrimage into a residential experience is one important way of opening the spiritual to the secular. And here, the tragedy of the Reformation is all too plain; cathedrals have lost their monks (or at least those that were monastic foundations have), and therefore much of their ability to provide hospitality to pilgrims and strangers. A strong case can be made for cathedrals to develop residential communities, places where people can come to stay for a day, a week, a month or longer. Such residential communities can help to develop the cathedral's own spirituality, and to provide hospitality for those whom God brings to them.

Many come simply because the cathedral, in virtue of its considerable resources, is one of the nation's greatest patrons of the arts. A cathedral choir is often an internationally recognized art form, living art whose importance transcends the spiritual nature of its task, and whose members are as important as the paint on the Picasso or the bronze of the Frink sculpture. Cathedral music often extends well beyond the ritual of Sunday worship, creating the opportunity for local, national and international orchestras to perform both sacred and secular works in a setting that echoes the prayer and spirituality of generations before us. Imaginatively used, the resources of cathedral music can inspire the development of links with local schools, the creation of music scholarships, the participation of leading instrumentalists in the development of local musicians. It is this kind of contact, employing the skills and ambitions of local people, and providing them with excellent opportunities to participate for reasons other than faith, that builds bridges for those who belong by association.

In the same way, cathedrals can act as an inspiration to the visual arts, creating surprising places of spiritual challenge by using both sculptures and paintings to transform fixed ideas and to help people to experience the creativity, joy, pain and sheer 'otherness' of the sacred. This use of art as a form of challenge, as a route to prayer, and as a means of creating a new spiritual identity, is one of the most exciting developments in cathedral ministry in the past fifty or sixty years. Chichester Cathedral was foundational in this process before and during the last war; in rediscovering the role of art in the development of spirituality, those cathedrals that have followed its example have helped to inform and nurture the beliefs and faith of many thousands of people who have no formal or participative allegiance to any Christian community, but who nevertheless are challenged and humbled by the expression of the cross within the art of those who have been prepared to take the risk of challenging our traditional understanding of Christianity. But the creation of Christian art is not merely a challenge to the viewer; it can challenge and change the artist as well. So from choir members to painters, sculptors to musicians, artists can develop their art in an environment that speaks of the transcendence and immanence of God.

So accessibility, openness, architecture, and the voice of art and music all help to enable the kind of experience of spirituality that is not only beyond the ability of the parish church, but has of late been outside its participative theology. But there is a much more fundamental role that cathedrals can play in crossing the boundaries between traditional Christianity, of which they are supreme exponents, and the different spiritualities of today's culture. Their role in inter-faith development, particularly if they can allow members of other religious traditions to create ritual dialogue within their boundaries, is enormously important. Through the careful appointment of staff who are theologically competent and sufficiently at ease with their own faith not to worry too much about the risk of working with other religious traditions, they can create centres of spiritual learning that set out quite deliberately to deconstruct the barriers that some have erected between Christianity and other faith communities. The energy of these ancient buildings, resting on centuries of daily prayer and eucharistic worship, can help to drive forward a gentle dialogue that people of all spiritual traditions can enter, and by doing so, they can create precisely the kind of environment that Christians whose faith is formed, not by participation in local congregations but by their own reading, study and personal pilgrimage, need to help them to grow. Cathedrals are, by nature, the most classic example of a centre set theology, allowing people of all spiritualities to explore, without criticism or expectation, the Christ who is at the heart of the universe.

This centre set theology is one that can become a model for the local parish church as it seeks effectively to fulfil its role as the spiritual centre of its community. But so often, one of the enduring legacies of the cathedral is its culture of control. Cathedral chapters have, in the past, been very much a law unto themselves, and have created a fortress mentality that has not been healthy either for their members, or for the wider community. The recent changes in the way that cathedrals are governed has yet to be tested, and the widening of the chapter to include lay canons is welcome, but the implications have yet to be fully realized. There remains a serious lack, not so much of democracy, because democracy is often a more shallow process than the embrace of the cross, but of engagement with those who come from the 'outside'. Lay members of the chapter are drawn, naturally, from the members of the cathedral 'congregation' – those whose normal place of worship is the cathedral itself – and these people tend to be from the more conservative wing of the Church's life, and certainly not from those who are occasional associate members. Thus the representation on the cathedral chapter of those for whom the cathedral is most equipped to provide a centre of worship and spirituality, those who belong by association rather than participation, is likely to be non-existent. And the ability of the new structures of cathedral government to appreciate the unique role of the cathedral will remain uncertain for many years yet. The desire to bring the bishop into a closer relationship of responsibility is also a two-edged sword; while it might bring the cathedral closer to the work of the diocese, it might also reinforce the participative element in cathedral life to the detriment of one of the cathedral's greatest gifts – the ability to create a centre set theology that provides, on the one hand, one of the richest examples of Christian worship and ritual, and on the other, a totally open approach to people who might come from a variety of spiritual backgrounds, and certainly not from the conservative wing of the *corpus Anglicana*.

The role of the cathedral in providing a liturgical and ritual experience that can be extended beyond its immediate congregation through radio, television and the Internet should not be limited simply to presenting the richness of its Christian tradition. By opening itself to the experience of other spiritualities, the cathedral can help to create that all-important dialogue between people of different spiritual paths. Many Druids, for example, consider the cathedrals of our nation to be powerful places of spirituality, and as such, feel as much owners of them as Christians. Those who come from the Asian spiritualities can often relate to the cathedral as a temple in a way that they cannot to a closely guarded, 'closed set' parish church. But the hidden heart of the cathedral is in its residential community. Whether it is the Augustinian canons, with their common rule of life, or the canons as Reformation replacements for the Benedictine monks, the expanded residential community that today embraces more than the dean and canons, often including the musicians, administrators, educators and visiting theologians, can form the basis for a yet wider community of exploration.

This wider community needs residence. It may be that in developing programmes of spiritual awareness, or in helping people to appreciate the art or music of the place, cathedrals can use the resources of the cathedral city in providing this residence. Guest houses, hotels, even the possible use of the retreat house, all are options. But none of them come close to participation in the residential life of a worshipping community over a number of days. A recent conversation I had with the abbot of Burford, Stuart Burns, illustrates this point. His guest house is usually full with retreatants, people who have come to share the life of the monastery. Some of them are oblates, members of the third order of the Benedictine community. But the abbot has closed the oblature, not because he doesn't receive sufficient applications, but because he receives too many. From his point of view, it is the only thing he can do, because the community simply cannot cope with the number of people who want to belong to it; he would be swamped. Yet in a culture that is used to market forces and a demand-driven economy, the action of shutting off your market simply because demand has become too great is an act of monumental folly. And it is here that the cathedrals can come into their own. What is to stop them offering a 'third order' attached to the worshipping life of the cathedral? A whole host of exciting possibilities would develop, not least the demand for residential accommodation within the confines of the cathedral. The regular pattern of morning, midday and evening prayer, coupled with work given freely to the cathedral, would be an attractive proposition to a host of people, many of whom belong to no parish congregation, many of whom would be precisely the associate members that we need to support. Already the beginnings of such communities are emerging. Wells Cathedral, for example, holds residential courses on spirituality. Norwich Cathedral has held Benedictine experience weeks. But these things are merely the beginnings, the first buds of a spring that is yet to come. There is a vast amount of social evidence that our cathedrals are scratching where people itch: attendance figures are considerably higher than they were ten years ago, programmes of music, spirituality, and new, creative acts of worship run alongside the daily round of traditional worship; and people are increasingly seeing cathedrals as resources for the development of an even wider ministry of new and traditional spirituality. But I strongly believe that they can only really begin to develop this potential if they can find ways of developing the kind of residence that allows people to come and stay within their communities, to take time out for a day, or a week, or a month, to immerse themselves in the spiritual and worshipping life of the community from within, and as part of the daily working life of the cathedral.

Curiously, those who belong by association are much more willing to participate in a meaningful way by residence than they are through the weekly round of parish life. Just as people with little or no participative experience of the local church will delight in a pilgrimage to Iona or Taizé, so too will they be found in the guest houses of our monasteries and convents. It is part of our culture to concentrate on specific periods for self-improvement. We go on 'courses' for this and that, so it shouldn't surprise us when people want to spend a week or so engaging with their spirituality. The successful Alpha Courses are built on this premise. And there is something about cathedral life that also preserves the integrity of distance, something that allows us to maintain a 'critical distance' from both the heart of the faith, and from the ritual community that preserves it and from which we wish to learn. That 'critical distance' is not so easy when one is a part of a parish, with its much more closely knit life and its expectation of long-term involvement. And somehow, within a parish, unless it is one of those rare and valuable breeds of centre set community, any kind of critical analysis, any attempt at exploration or experimentation, can be perceived as challenge, as counter-culture. Withdrawal and privacy are more difficult. Engagement is the prevailing mind-set of the average parish. Yet the creation of sacred space within communities is one of the most important things that we can do, allowing people to explore their spirituality without the 'oughts' and 'ought nots' of traditional congregational life. The creation of residence within the confines of the cathedral close, as part of the warp and weft of cathedral life, could provide both sacred space and tranquillity for those who are starved of the sacred in daily life, and overworked by the sheer and unremitting pace of the secular.

That the cathedral has a county role is well established. It is host to a whole range of special services for this and that, from Young Farmers (where they still exist) to county memorial services, from public school confirmations to annual services for the Royal and Ancient Order of Buffalos. But its county role can work against its emerging role as a centre for spiritual development precisely because the former role is such a demanding and fragmented one. The task of holding all these disparate elements of county and national life together, of praying for them and helping them to relate to each other, is vitally important, but it can drain the cathedral of its space and continuity, which are two of its most important resources for outsiders. When the cathedral is shut to visitors and pilgrims because of a special service, which role is it fulfilling, and which is it denying? When the visitor complains that he or she can't get in to pray, or simply to stand and drink in the energy and spirituality of the place, is it right to say that the cathedral is engaged in its primary purpose, or is the visitor correct in feeling somehow shut out and rejected from his or her proper right of access? And how does the depth of feeling about charging for cathedral entrance resonate with this sense that the cathedral is a sacred space, open for all who wish to come? Perhaps we should recognize that the primary purpose of the cathedral is to create a sacred space within which worship is offered, and which makes no demands on those who come to experience it beyond the demands of the sacred itself.

Dialogue with the casual visitor can be a creative way of using the richer resources of the cathedral, and many have recognized this by the appointment of diocesan clergy to help as 'honorary chaplains'. Many retired clergy are only too happy to give time to meet the visitors who come in their thousands, to pray with those who need prayer, and to help people approach the faith 'crabwise', from a new direction or with an unexpected idea. Stand in any of our great cathedral churches and watch the visitors, and you will soon recognize that for most, the call of the sacred is interpreted in looking at the architecture rather than the purpose of the place. Unlike a visit to an Asian temple, where people come with a clear idea of offering sacrifice to the ancestors, or bringing gifts for the priests, or seeking a propitious time for some family event, a visit to an English cathedral often ends up being a slightly puzzled tour of the tombstones and architecture. We are somehow embarrassed by our spirituality, and find it difficult to engage the visitor in the sacred. Perhaps we are wise to let the building's energy and the stones immersed in the prayers of the ages do its own job, yet I can't help feel that we are missing something. A nation that can respond to a road crash by leaving flowers at the crash site, by lighting candles at the place of death, is not a society that is shy of ritual or the markers of the sacred. Maybe we need to be more open about the core purpose of the cathedral, inviting visitors to experience the silence of meditative prayer or the ritual of offering as part of the tour. Some cathedrals do attempt this, but there is often a sense of embarrassment about the process, as if somehow we were inviting strangers into our bedroom.

The recognition of deep spirituality in great art and music is one of the gifts that cathedrals can give to the nation. The maintenance of cathedral choirs – by no means an inexpensive business in today's culture of professionalism – is only one aspect of this spirituality. Many have found the resources to commission works of art that are at least as effective as a sermon in touching the spiritual core of the casual visitor. In Gloucester Cathedral, for example, there is a single rough-hewn stone in the centre of the south transept. It makes its own statement, raising questions and bringing into focus the stuff from which the whole building has been made. It creates a link between the worship of the building and the sacredness of creation itself. In front of the north entrance to Wells Cathedral there are carvings representing the four Gospels. The purpose of art, and specifically of religious art, is to challenge us, to shake us out of the recognized patterns of religion and to take us into areas where we have feared to tread, even sometimes to shock us by exposing the ugliness or the violence of our own lives. Always it will raise questions. And it can do so without words, without portentous declarations from raised pulpits. Great art can challenge, can literally revolutionize, without doing anything other than simply being there.

The opportunity for cathedrals to become experimental laboratories for new kinds of worship is enormous. They have the space, the distance and the resources to do things that parish churches cannot. They can take risks, because they do not have the immediate worry of losing a participant congregation and the finance that goes with it. They can engage with a much larger community than a parish church can, and they can do so in a framework of quiet Christian confidence that does not shout or draw inappropriate attention to itself. With careful thought, they can provide the kind of resources for those who belong by association that the local parish church cannot. Lectures, concerts, dances, theatre, exhibitions – all are possible within the space of the cathedral. The content of these can be as challenging and as various as the imagination of their chapters. They are the ultimate 'safe space' in which to create new ways of experiencing God.

Chapter 9

Media and Mission

If the Church has the task of reaching beyond its doors to those who belong by association, it has in today's western media culture a tremendous opportunity to engage with them. Over 90 per cent of the population in the United Kingdom owns a television. That means that nearly everyone has access to one, or has seen a television programme during the past week. Despite the drop in reading ability, newspapers still sell well, the circulation of the *News of the World* (4.1 million), the *Sun* (3.5 million) and the *Daily Telegraph* (1 million) running into millions of copies each week. Local and regional newspapers have a considerable impact, and the range and variety of consumer magazines is stunning. Radio can also reach a massive audience: BBC Radio 4's flagship current affairs programme, *Today*, has a national audience and often sets the news agenda for the day. There is a host of local, independent and specialist radio stations competing for attention, many of which gain considerable local following and loyalty.

The delivery of these media has expanded rapidly since the original terrestrial broadcast system – using a local transmitter to beam a signal to the TV aerial on a roof. Direct satellite broadcasting, where a signal is sent via satellite to an individual satellite dish and receiver on a house, has become a vast business, in which BSkyB dominates the UK market. The BBC has expanded into direct satellite broadcasting, and has invested millions in this new delivery system.

At the same time as direct satellite broadcasting was expanding, in the mid-1980s, cable companies were competing to achieve the vision of interconnectivity. It was one of the dreams of the latter years of the Thatcher government, taken on into the rump years of John Major's administration, that every house should be 'wired' with cable. The dream was, as usual, consumer-led, based on the idea that if every house were 'wired', we could all order our consumable goods from the comfort of our television screens. The fact that the Government removed the requirement for planning permission, so that cable companies could win franchises to dig up our streets and lanes to lay the ubiquitous green pipes that would carry the fibre-optic cables wherever and however they liked, meant that a number of companies (mostly US and Dutch) invested heavily in pipe-laying. Not all of the pipes were wired, but in the heavily populated parts of the country, and particularly those parts where socio-economic groups B and C1 were concentrated, wiring went ahead fiercely in the late 1980s and early to mid-1990s. It continues to this day, but with the growing realization that because technology has developed rapidly, and the amount of data that can be pumped through the fibre-optic cables has also expanded, we are enormously over-cabled. We currently use only a few per cent of the current cable capacity between the USA and Europe. But what started out as a telephone and television revolution, with the idea of 'piping in' television programmes that would use the telephone line to create interactive shopping, has turned into an Internet revolution, the pipes being used increasingly to bring high-speed broadband Internet connections to our homes.

And so these three 'traditional' media, television, newspapers and radio, while accounting for massive audiences by themselves, have been joined by a fourth that has all but revolutionized the communications industry – the Internet. The growth of worldwide computer-mediated communication has had a major impact on the way we get our information. All school children are trained to use the Internet as a matter of Government policy, most classrooms having access in some way. Colleges and universities have access through the giant academic network, and students are given e-mail accounts as part of their induction. Education is being revolutionized by the introduction of Internet learning – not only by students individually looking up information on the net, but by the sharing of classroom teaching remotely via the Internet. Nearly every organization that wants to be serious about its presence in today's communication culture will have its own website, and those concerned about their customer relations will increasingly develop an Internet community of members – creating a virtual network of people who use their products or who are interested in the issues with which they deal.

The result is that for many people, the Internet, and particularly the World Wide Web, has become the first stop not only for information, but also for community. Search engines that enable the billions of pages of information on the Web to be searched by topic, subject or keyword have made it possible to get information about almost anything in a matter of seconds. Alongside this 'one-stop' information and data retrieval, virtual communities have developed, in which people with similar interests from various parts of the world have been able to discuss them, or to share information. Some of the content, from a Christian perspective, has been less than healthy, and it is true to say that pornography was the principal driver of this new technology in the early days – so much so, in fact, that while the Internet service providers have made public statements about cleaning up the network, they continue to use implicit (and sometimes explicit) references to sexuality in their advertising[1]. There are serious theological issues to be raised here that are outside the scope of this book, though some of them have been touched on in the earlier discussion about disintermediation. Suffice it to say that the Internet is an extremely important development for any organization wishing to reach its audiences; and for the Church, it provides a major opportunity not only for the dissemination of information, but also for the development of virtual communities.

Yet the churches' take-up of these opportunities, either in the 'traditional' media of television, newspapers and radio, or in the new media of the Internet, has been at best slow and poorly funded. In the early days of radio, the churches became involved, particularly when the BBC copied the phenomenal success of the pirate radio stations and established the local radio network. These local stations initially managed to create community involvement, with the education, sports and religious affairs producers being seconded or subsidized by their respective audiences. However, the increasing 'professionalization' of the BBC has led to the disappearance of these secondments. Where they still exist, they live in uneasy cohabitation with the full-time 'professional' journalists and producers. The Church was never fully able to adapt its budgeting to support them anyway, and many lived on very low wages. When the Churches' Media Trust was formed in 1991, it found that the Oxford Council of Churches was paying the religious producer for BBC Radio Oxford the princely sum of £4,000 per annum for a half-time post. The Trust set itself the task of putting this injustice to rights. Raising money from local congregations to increase the stipend to the equivalent of a BBC staff producer was relatively easy, as they saw (and heard) the value of this contribution. But the reaction of the Church structures was typical of its lack of vision and investment. The Diocese of Oxford promptly cut its grant, letting the Trust carry the entire weight of funding.

In the event, this was not much of a problem, because the Trust argued, along with many within the BBC, that the Church should not be contributing financially to the BBC for its religious programming. The Church was, in effect, paying twice: once through the licence fee paid by most of its members, and again through donations that could well be spent elsewhere. For the BBC's part, it was uneasy taking money from external religious groups, because it believed (correctly) that its impartiality was threatened.

Many bishops saw this cosy arrangement as vital in maintaining the presence of the Church within the BBC. They failed to grasp the single most important fact of broadcasting: that the Church is news simply by being faithful to the prophetic voice of the gospel. We should not need to 'pay our way in'; in fact, this was and is a highly counter-productive approach for many reasons. And for the BBC, the removal of these 'specialist' broadcasters meant that, possibly for the first time, fairly junior broadcast journalists on the staff of the stations were having to grapple with religious issues, where before they had simply shunted them into the pigeonhole of the local vicar who came in to produce the 'God slot'. While this has occasionally led to some hilarious conversations between church communicators and radio journalists as they explore new territory, the overall effect of the removal of this superficially cosy relationship has been beneficial to both sides.

The difficulty that the Church has today in making an effective impact in the huge and diverse media culture is not primarily structural or financial. It is theological and spiritual. At heart, we find it hard to take the risk of speaking the truth, of saying what we believe is demanded by our fellowship with the crucified God, and prefer the safety of approval. We are afraid of the risk of speaking uncomfortable truths. Perhaps the journalists will oppose us publicly, or worse, will make us feel bad when we have to face those who disagree with us. Those most effectively equipped to make an impact in today's media – the future leaders of the Church – are those most tempted to pull their punches because of the fear of what honesty and truth-speaking might do to their future careers. To deal with this problem we have to go to the heart of what it means to embrace the cross. To have died with Christ means to have no fear of what life can do with us and to us. It is to place ourselves in the hands of our God, without equivocation. It is only as we begin to take seriously the death of the one who calls us to follow him that we can engage in a truly Christian way with the community within which we live, and the media that inform it.

But there is also an ambivalence at the heart of our relationship with the media that needs to be acknowledged and expressed. Where communication media have been used to strengthen the supportive relationships between individuals and communities, or to increase mutual understanding, it has brought great benefits. News and current affairs programmes that increase our understanding of those who differ from us are highly welcome. Internet connectivity has helped to bring us nearer to each other, and has the potential to increase freedom of thought and discussion. Great drama, for example, like other great art, can inspire and move us. But much of the visual and printed media plays to the darker side of our nature. The erosion of spiritual values by the media's globalization of western secularism poses a real problem to places like India and Africa. The amount of time that our own children spend watching television has become a threat to their physical well-being, as well as dulling their innate spiritual awareness. The modern phenomenon of the surrogate community, the 'soap opera', has serious consequences for those of us that are concerned with the transmission of values through shared symbols and ritual. And increasingly, the printed media find their identity and their sales figures through the strident affirmation of the very worst of our emotions. We are stridently encouraged to distrust the asylum seeker in our midst, or to envy the support they get, or worse, to deny them the compassion they deserve. We are saturated by advertising that treats us and our children merely as consumers, and that promotes an unrealistic Disney-like world where only the beautiful succeed. It would not hurt us to abandon the media for more intimate forms of communication, such as inviting our neighbours to supper or engaging more directly with the asylum seeker in our midst.

This ambivalence makes it difficult for the Church to engage effectively with the media, because it divides our engagement between a search for relevance and a challenge to values. But the search for relevance which some parts of the Church have become increasingly preoccupied with is a false search. We don't become relevant by seeking relevance. We become relevant precisely because we have abandoned the search for relevance and have turned instead to embrace the cross. This embrace will lead us to lose ourselves in the service of our neighbours. It will lead us to prayer instead of action when the world looks for action, and it will lead us to action when the world would rather we did nothing, except perhaps pray. But it is only when we have recognized that approval by the world is a dangerous path that leads to the loss of spiritual life, and when we have tasted the exhilarating freedom of following Christ without worrying about his relevance to the news agenda or the popularity of discipleship, that we will be truly free to make an impact on the world through the media. Very often, the task of the Church is to tell people what they don't want to hear.

Models of Communication

The aim of the Church when dealing with the media, and of the individual Christians and Christian communities within it, must be to use the opportunities it presents to offer a transformational model of discipleship to those amongst whom we live. Transformation is not the only model for communication. It is perfectly possible to see the media merely as means of imparting information. Offering the media information about forthcoming events, or the success of the latest fund-raising programme, is in itself helpful, and necessary to demonstrate the presence and life of the Church. But it is not, by itself, sufficient. Jesus didn't spend time in the marketplace offering information about God. He engaged in dialogue. He challenged behaviour and created stories that helped to draw people into an engagement with the living God. He met with them in their homes, their places of work, their families, their illness and their anxiety.

At the other end of the spectrum, it is too easy today to copy the 'spin-doctoring' approach of the political parties (and indeed almost every other contemporary institution or organization) in creating a model that has more to do with propaganda than with transformation. By definition, propaganda is the use of distorted information to manipulate the behaviour of others. It is alien to the gospel, and should never be used by Christians. Yet the distinction between a model of communication based on propaganda and one based on transformation is sometimes difficult to discern in the way that the Church uses the media. The essence of a transformational model of communication is the desire to create dialogue; to challenge the individual, or the community, to examine its behaviour or its beliefs and to look in new ways at believing or behaving.

You can tell that a communication model is information-driven because it will concentrate almost exclusively on the organization or institution. It will rarely present a challenge to the structures around it or the individuals it disagrees with. Part of the difficulty of the Church of England's communication over the past twenty years is that it has been driven in no small part by an information model, and has used the public media for internal communications. Indeed, as an institution, its internal communication processes are so chaotic that it has no alternative but to use the public media as a means of internal dialogue. It desperately needs to recover a model of communication that is transformational.

One of the finest examples of a transformational model of communication is the parable. Jesus told these stories not in order to make an analogy, but to create an internal dialogue within his hearers. They were seeds, planted in the hearts of his hearers, that if allowed to grow, would lead to a re-examination and a fresh evaluation of the nature of God and his world. The point at which the surprise and the challenge emerge is the point of germination. Take the parable of the Good Samaritan (Luke 10.29–37) as a key example. The surprise comes when you discover that it was not the priest, nor the Levite, but the hated Samaritan who stops and cares for the injured man. The challenge comes in the concluding phrase 'go and do thou likewise'. To exhort his hearers to follow someone who is, according to Jewish thinking, theologically mistaken and culturally deficient is a fine example of turning the tables on the questioner who asked 'And who is my neighbour?' Jesus' answer is that my neighbour is anyone who needs my care.

So a transformational model of communication will not be as much concerned with explaining as with creating internal questions, questions that will sometimes lead to public debate, sometimes to quiet reflection, and sometimes simply to personal rejection because the issues they raise are too painful. And this is not entirely a human activity; the activity of the Spirit, at work in those who speak and those who hear, is as important as the act of communication itself. But the alternatives are inadequate for a fully Christian understanding of communication. Unless we are prepared to risk the loss of identity and relevance through the embrace of the cross, we can never speak clearly to those who listen through the print, broadcast and computer media.

Thus transformation is not simply something that happens to our readers, our listeners or our viewers. It is an internal process that happens to us as well. As we take Christian discipleship seriously, we become differentiated from the world in which we live, but not isolated from it. Instead of seeking relevance and identity by being the same as our neighbours, we seek to define ourselves by the values of the Kingdom of God, risking the loss of relevance and identity. The curious paradox is that as we continue to take the risk of identity with Christ, we become different in a way that creates interest, stimulates questions and demands attention. We become relevant and interesting to the media not because we are the same, but because the way we think and act offers a different solution to the problems faced by our fellow human beings.

Using the media in this way will allow us to engage more effectively with those who belong by association. If most of our communication is about the Church's internal processes or politics, then those who have no wish to engage in this way will find it all a bit irrelevant. But if we can use the direct and personal engagement of the media to address critical issues, to challenge injustice and to affirm creativity, this will have an immediate appeal to those who believe but don't belong.

How then does all of this work in the parish, in the local Christian congregation or community? The first step is to recognize that the community to which we speak, and for whom we care, is much wider than our participating membership. As the parable of the Good Samaritan suggests, it is to recognize that our neighbour is the one who needs our attention, our care and our love, no matter how alienated he or she may be in other ways. Our neighbour is not simply the person who attends our church, but the unknown teenager who sits on the wall outside the church, the mother struggling to feed and clothe her children on an inadequate wage, or the wealthy businessman weighed down with anxiety and fear. We are called not only to speak to all of them, but to bring them into a new relationship with God, and for this we need different media for different audiences. For those who are already in our churches, the sermon or house-group will be an excellent medium because there is no communication that is more effective than one individual relating to another. But for those who do not participate, but who nevertheless belong to God, if not to us, we have to use the wider media.

The traditional print and broadcast media offer a good platform for this. The key thing to remember, when talking to journalists, is that we are speaking through them to their audience. If they are doing their job properly, they will be representative people, representing the audience for whom they write or broadcast. So a dialogue with the journalist is, in essence, a dialogue with those people we wish to reach. The aim is not simply to give them information, and certainly not to manipulate the story to our own ends by giving partial or distorted information; it is to seek to engage the reader or listener in the sacred dialogue between the heart of God and the heart of his children. There is absolutely no need to feel a victim in this relationship. The journalist may, or may not, have his or her own agenda, and that agenda may or may not intrude into the interview. But the journalist has come to us for a comment, an opinion, or to clarify the facts. In each of these cases, we are put into the position of expert. For the brief three minutes of a radio interview, or the paragraph of the newspaper, we can take full responsibility for what we say because we have been asked for our views or our understanding of the facts. There is no need to apologize for the gospel, especially if the language and shape of the interview is couched in secular language. Paradoxically, it is when our humanity is most exposed that our spirituality can be most effective. Of course, all the practical skills of writing a press release, being interviewed by a radio or print journalist, knowing what makes a good news story, being aware of the potential of the visual aspects of a story for television – all of this is important, and there are plenty of training organizations who will equip individuals with the necessary skills. There is no excuse for sloppy and unprofessional communication. But no matter how professional we might be, without the prophetic life of the Spirit we will never be able to do more than scratch the surface of our readers' or listeners' attention.

If the first step in implementing a cohesive communication strategy is one of attitude – recognizing that those with whom we engage in dialogue include those who never come to our churches – then the next step is developing practical ways of nourishing and developing the relationship we have with them. The constant and regular (even if not frequent) presence in the local print and broadcast media will create a climate of awareness on which to build, but there needs to be a network of supportive links into the heart of the spiritual life of our church that can act as channels of dialogue and communication. The best and most effective of these are the participant members of the church itself, because there is nothing better for conveying the life of the Spirit than human contact in its vulnerability and honesty. For centre set congregations, this will be a relatively uncontroversial step to take, even if it is a difficult and challenging one. The idea that each of us is capable of joining a spiritual pilgrimage, and that many of us have been on the journey for a long time, whether or not we are members of a church, will be a well-known concept. The discussion of spirituality, and the presence of rituals, signs and symbols of the sacred, will be as natural as breathing. But for closed set churches, the danger will be that the participant members will have a propagandist approach to those outside their church; they will see relationships solely in terms of conversion, and will miss the gentle but effective 'walking alongside' that so typifies the ministry of the risen Lord.

The Internet also opens up massive opportunities for the local congregation. We need to move away from an external communication strategy based entirely on the parish magazine. Granted, the magazine is vital; it works at a number of levels. First, it provides a constant presence, reflecting the life of the congregation. Second, it provides information. Most important, it can provide an entry point into the dialogue between the sacred and the secular, bringing associate members into contact with participant members through the printed word. But in today's culture of computer-mediated communication, the parish magazine cannot and should not stand on its own. It can be supplemented and supported by the use of the Internet.

A parish does not have to jump immediately to the creation of a website. E-mail is a very good starting point. It is perfectly possible to put together an e-mail containing the key points of the Sunday notice sheet, including a brief comment on the readings and possibly a very, very brief outline of the sermon, and send it to those people who have signed up to receive it. By publishing a notice in the parish magazine and the Sunday notice sheet inviting people with e-mail to contact the vicar (or whoever takes on this ministry) if they want a weekly e-mail about the life of the church, it is possible to extend the ministry of the magazine and the Sunday notice sheet quite considerably. Such an e-mail list can be built up over time, creating a regular weekly network of people receiving news and information about the church. Some of those will be people who live a considerable distance away from the church, and such e-mail links can reinforce their sense of belonging and educate their spirituality considerably.

But an electronic mailing list really comes into its own when it is combined with a parish website. It is relatively easy for a parish to create at least a one-page site. It can cost very little, and even if the church leaders lack the skills required, they can usually and with great effect find someone in the congregation willing to undertake the design and construction of one. The web page should have, as a bare minimum, the location of the church, the times of its principal services, the contact address and telephone number of the minister, and the principal interests and activities of its members. But it can also have a form for visitors to submit their e-mail address so that they can subscribe (and unsubscribe) to the weekly information sheet. The presence of a page or two of Web information on the Internet will soon be noticed by the various search engines, whose 'spiders' crawl around the millions of pages, harvesting information for the search engines to use. St Mary's Church, Fiddlington will be noticed, and all sorts of people will log on to the web page to find information. Many of them will be those who feel they have some link with the church. They may be visiting Fiddlington, wanting to know the times of Sunday worship. They may have relatives there, or be members of the local community who go to the Internet as the first place to look for information. By inviting them to subscribe to a weekly information sheet, an electronic mailing list can quickly be established. The beauty of such a mailing list is that one gets maximum return for minimum extra energy. The cost and time involved in sending one e-mail or a hundred e-mails is the same, and is minimal. Most of the copy will already be available, because it will appear in either the Sunday notice sheet or the parish magazine. And the work of gathering and maintaining the list is minimal, particularly if it is coupled with an automatic subscribe and unsubscribe process. The key to making this kind of list work is to make sure it is regular, and that it is sent out at the same time each week or each month. When combined with a website, the most that is needed is a brief description and a link to the site. Put the bulk of the material on the website, send a brief description with a link to that particular page to those on the mailing list, and you have an excellent form of communication that will considerably reinforce people's sense of belonging.

There are also dangers in this process, because the opportunities presented for engagement and communication can provide the Church with the same kind of 'controlling' opportunities that some of the national media have espoused. We have to use these new media wisely, and this will mean providing an opportunity for disagreement and dialogue. In any healthy community there will be many people who will disagree on both the specifics of an issue and the broad position. The level of encouragement for debate and discussion of such differences is a very real measure of the health of a community. The new communication opportunities can be used as much to encourage the sharing of diverse and differing opinions as for providing information. It is when they are used to promote one view or one theological position that they become most alienating for those who disagree. Just as we need to welcome centre set communities, so too do we need to encourage centre set communications.

So the Internet comes into its own when it includes opportunities for its users to engage in dialogue. It is also very useful in providing access to occasional activities. For example, a visit to the Taizé community or an occasional seminar on business ethics might be very attractive to someone who would not hear about it otherwise, because he or she is not a participant member of the church. Offering a line or two about the opportunity or issues, and linking to a website where fuller information is available, saves you time in writing and saves the reader time because they can skip quickly to those things that interest them.

The process can be developed further by making sure that you include, as a subsection of your e-mail list, a list of the local journalists and media outlets. Sending them a copy of the e-mail link will usually result in at least one story in the local media, and will create yet another connection with your community for which you have had to do very little work!

The deliberate creation of a community of those who belong by association through the use of the Internet, and particularly by the creation of mailing lists, gives us a useful insight into the nature of the community that wishes to relate to us. Such a community will, of course, be limited to those who use the new technology. Many who belong by association do not or cannot afford it, so such a process is at best partial. But it is important, and perhaps for the first time can give us a clue to the scope, geographical spread and size of our associate membership.

In a similar way, the use of the parish magazine – especially if paid for – can give a similar indication. As a rough rule of thumb, I have discovered that the circulation of an average paid-for parish magazine for an Anglican church is roughly 1.8 times the size of the electoral roll if it is fully marketed. So for a church with an electoral roll of 150, the target circulation should be around 280. Any more, and the magazine is doing very well. Any less, and there is probably capacity to expand the circulation a bit. This, in itself, gives an indication of the size of what is often called the 'fringe' membership. But as we noted earlier, the definition of 'fringe' is contentious, and in any case may not correspond to the larger 'associate' membership.

So far, our understanding of the use of the media has been driven by the unchallenged assumption that it is the Church who holds the core teaching of the Christian faith and in an ideal world uses all the means at its disposal, including the media, to transmit that core teaching to those who wish to hear or learn. In effect, we believe that it is the Church's task to be the 'story keeper'. But in an age of media domination, where stories are valued for their own pulling power, is this assumption entirely correct? There is considerable evidence to suggest that the media, used both as entertainment and as an educational tool in schools, has a much wider and far more central role than the Church normally allows.

In 1990, the Revd Brian Brown, former Head of Religious Studies at Lady Spencer Churchill College (then part of Oxford Polytechnic, now part of Oxford Brookes University), decided that he would produce a cartoon series, called *Story-Keepers*, that would retell the stories of the Gospels from that period of the Church's life after the early apostolic age recorded in Acts, but before the Gospels were completed. In other words, he would depict the transmission of the Gospel stories by word of mouth using cartoon characters created to show how things might have been. Each episode tells the story of Ben, a baker, and his wife, Helena, who are Christians in Rome at the time Emperor Nero was persecuting them (AD 64). Ben and Helena have adopted four children whose parents were lost during the fires set by Nero. Jesus' hope-giving stories and parables are told in the course of their exciting adventures.

When *Story-Keepers* was screened on Independent Television on a Sunday morning, it beat the Disney cartoons that followed by a huge margin. It got an audience of 1.4 million, 29 per cent of the audience share, and reached 49 per cent of all four to nine-year-olds watching television at that time.

So the belief that the Church is the primary story-teller and transmitter of the Gospel stories, certainly in numerical terms and possibly in creative and dynamic terms, is now mistaken. The media and education form between them a much larger and more potent 'story-telling' body than the Church can ever hope to become. This is something that many Church leaders find difficult to accept. Much of the main thrust of

117

policy, at least in the Church of England, and possibly in the more Evangelical mainstream denominations, has been to preserve the Church's role as guardian of the faith, even when this results in the denial of creative opportunities for retelling the stories. Take, for example, the rejection of those who come to the Church for rites of passage. In confining the role of the Church in taking marriage services to those who have not had any previous marital relationship, the Church not only denies its central message – that of repentance, forgiveness and restoration – but also misses a golden opportunity to create the kind of relationships that enable the stories to be retold. Yet the stories have a life of their own, driven by the Spirit that empowers them, and the Church is often caught on the back foot as it finds itself reduced to a mere commentator on the presentation of those stories by groups and organizations that own no allegiance to bishops, nor sit under any authority apart from the creative and dynamic power of the stories themselves. And the media present an ideal culture within which those stories can flourish.

Take, for example, the reworking of the themes of sacrifice and redemption in the Harry Potter series. Condemned by many on the Evangelical wing of the mainstream churches because of their apparent focus on witchcraft and wizardry, these stories in fact re-create all the main biblical themes of membership of a covenant community, the fight against evil, and the central importance and utter, harsh necessity of personal sacrifice as a core element of that fight, with Harry's parents paying the ultimate penalty for resistance against the darker powers of evil. These themes have crossed all the media boundaries, from their initial publication in book form, through film, to Internet and computer games. Yet the narrow concept that Christian belief must involve belonging to a particular Christian community that is defined by a particular doctrine and a particular ritual has rendered much of the Church impotent and unable to respond creatively to this powerful cultural reworking of the great Christian themes presented in the Harry Potter series. The fact that they are presented within a popular presentation of witchcraft should help, not hinder, Christian dialogue, because it is pagan spirituality that provides the most potent challenge to Christianity among young people in our secular and spiritually starved culture.

Here is the inevitable extension of the role of the media as story-keeper and story-teller. It lies not merely in the use of the film and television world by someone like Brian Brown, who at great cost to his health fought to bring the stories of the gospel to a wider audience by the use of the popular media; here, outside the Church, the fundamental power of the cross reasserts itself without any help from the Church, outside the drama of its liturgy or the control of its doctrine, simply because the cross, like gravity or special relativity, is part of how the world is made. And in order to respond to this natural discovery and recognition of the power of sacrifice and redemption in popular culture, the Church has to learn once again to abandon its struggle to preserve its identity, or its doctrinal purity, and engage in a mutual exploration of some of our culture's more popular myths.

The fact that the media are such powerful proponents of spirituality may be surprising to those whose main contact with it is through religious or pastoral controversy. Yet the struggle between good and evil, sacred and secular, redemption and fundamentalism, is played out in today's society not within the walls of the Church but on the screens of our televisions, in the pages of our newspapers, on our car radios and in the growing mountain of print in our newsagents and bookshops. That much of this is concerned with belief divorced entirely from belonging is not something to bewail, but something to celebrate and to engage with. The Church's preoccupation with personal salvation, with relevance and identity, has not equipped it to play a major role in our society; rather, it has created a timid, frightened Church that is more afraid of how it will appear in the media than how it can engage in dialogue with those who believe without belonging.

The debate about the Church's use of the media becomes almost completely sterile when it is simply about maintaining its position, or when it concentrates on how to keep its clergy producing local radio programmes, or how to maintain the preserved slots on Sunday television programming. The Christian community may be right to protest when it feels it is not getting a fair hearing, or when its beliefs and practices are distorted: this is an editorial issue, a programming issue. But much of its protest in the past ten years has been because the media have accurately portrayed it as an isolated, self-absorbed community that has lost its relevance precisely because it is so concerned with keeping it. As I have argued before, and will no doubt continue to argue, it is only when the Church is prepared to abandon its search for relevance and identity that it can begin to engage with the cross, to think creatively about its ministry, and to celebrate the discovery of the principles of repentance, sacrifice, forgiveness and redemption that are the main counterforce to the stark and destructive secular fundamentalism that destroys so much of our contemporary spirituality.

Ultimately, it is the recognition of Christian spirituality, even when this is covert, unrecognized, or unrelated to any sense of belonging to a Christian community, that enables the Church to engage with the media in an

effective way. As we enter the dialogue about, say, the place of Druid spirituality or the emphasis on sacrifice and redemption in the Harry Potter
books, we excite the interest of our fellow-creatures who are not sitting
in the pews Sunday by Sunday, but developing their understanding of
spirituality through the pages of the newspapers, or the dynamic of the
television programme. For this is how the media work. The listener or
viewer becomes an observer of the dialogue, engaging with it and
making up his or her mind about whether or not he or she agrees with
the points being made. By using the media to create dialogue, or to
engage creatively with discussion, rather than simply as a means to propa-
gate dogma, the Christian world-view can be rediscovered within the
culture of pop music, of soap opera, of news and current affairs. But the
prerequisite of dialogue is a willingness to embrace the other, to suffer the
loss of a previously valued identity, to be willing to be seen by some as
irrelevant because one is concerned with pursuing unpopular values or
breaking popular taboos. Dialogue cannot even begin if the starting
point is one of fixed positions. And this is precisely why so many people
reject membership of many Christian communities – because their experience of them is one of a lack of interest, and therefore a lack of
engagement, with the spiritual discoveries that are to them highly relevant
and extremely important. To be told at the outset that you are wrong, and
that your spiritual experience, while no doubt seeming true to you, is a
matter of delusion simply because it appears to contradict the received
dogmas of the Church, is literally to be excommunicated – rejected and
forced into the position of believing without belonging.

But dialogue is threatening to a Church that is not only afraid of the loss
of dogma, but also afraid of conflict. One of the most pervasive, but mistaken, paradigms embraced by many Church leaders is that Christian
leadership is about the avoidance or resolution of conflict. This is not
what one sees in the Gospels, or in the early Church. But years of the
'Gentle Jesus meek and mild' approach to Christianity has robbed some
of its leaders of the ability to disagree, to engage in conflict, and has rendered it impotent in the eyes of the media. Religious journalists who
occasionally get to know some of our Christian leaders often bewail the
fact that what they say in private is much sharper, more perceptive, ultimately more creative and redemptive, than anything they can be
persuaded to say in public. It is those religious leaders who are able, with
humility and compassion, to celebrate the conflict between, say, the liberal
and the fundamentalist agenda, and to enter into it by exposing the differences, rather than seeking always to find common ground, that are some of
our most effective apologists. But the 'fixed position' from which they

speak is that of the cross, rather than of dogma. And the cross is redemptive, forgiving, and above all, surprising, because it will find more common ground with the thief and the prostitute, or in today's culture possibly with the Druid and the Wiccan, than with the religious authorities of the day. It will be a position of true dialogue because it will be willing to be changed by the truth discovered by others, particularly those 'others' that the traditional communities of belief have rejected as 'outsiders', and it will also be willing to reject the posturing and false positions of those who have traditionally been called friends and fellow-travellers.

All this of course, is painful. But the cross always is. It always meets us with a challenge to sacrifice, and if resurrection and restoration are to be embraced, that challenge to sacrifice cannot be avoided. Thus the Church has to learn not so much to use the media as if they were tools at its disposal, but to engage with others through the media as a means of communication and dialogue. It has to be prepared to challenge, to enter into controversy, to take partial positions in order to discover new forms of relating. We will discover, if we are prepared for the pain of the encounter, that embracing the spirituality of those who belong by association, rather than participation, is an exciting and creative process that brings learning and wisdom to all those who take part, especially those who watch, listen to, or read about the encounter in today's media.

Chapter 10

Public Symbols and Private Rituals

If the hypothesis of this book – that there is a large number of people who belong to the Christian faith, and to the Church, by association rather than by participation – is accepted, then one of the most pressing questions that raises is how the Church can engage with them to inform and develop their faith. After all, if they don't participate in church services, come to house-groups, or read daily Bible notes, there don't seem to be many points of contact where the Church can engage with them. I have already suggested that the media are one resource the Church can use effectively to reinforce and develop the faith of those who belong by association. Apart from the media, perhaps the next most significant way those who belong by association (as well as those who belong by participation) can relate their faith to their daily life is through the use of public symbols and private rituals that create resonance and context for faith and give shape to its myths and doctrines. These symbols and rituals provide markers and contain teaching and stories that are essential, even in these days of mass media communication, for delineating the shape and dimensions of an individual and personal mental map of the sacred, and the helping to inform and give meaning to their beliefs. In fact, their use, when combined with the use of the media, can be highly effective.

All movements and institutions have their identifying symbols and be-havioural rituals, and they perform much the same tasks whatever the belief structures or behaviour patterns of the organization. First, they provide a means of identity for the members of the movement. From the modified handshake of the Masonic societies, through the hidden greeting of the fraternal society, to the more open display of a host of different badges by members of countless clubs and societies and the multi-million-pound market for the creators of logos and branding for public companies, the symbol provides an identity for its user that the organiza-tion works hard to ensure is unmistakable to the intended audience. Some brand symbols are known worldwide: McDonald's burger bars, Nike trainers, Guinness beer and Adidas sportswear are examples of brands, with their associated images, that are possibly better known around the world than the Christian cross.

Badges may be more than mere visual symbols. They can be verbal or visual formulae that press the buttons of recognition in particular groups of people. These formulae are often based on a certain kind of language. For example, the church that has a large notice board proclaiming 'Jesus is Lord' in Day-Glo paper is not simply making a statement of witness. The words and colours indicate that the church has a certain theology based on the Lordship of Jesus – it is certainly not a church that has a liberal theology or ministry, and it is unlikely to be Catholic or 'high church'. On the surface, the words appear to be a statement of witness to those 'outside' the Christian faith; in reality, they are more a signal to other Christians that a particular 'brand' of Christianity is to be found there. Not only does the notice signal a 'branding' to potential members, but it also provides reassurance to the current membership that they are part of a community of Christians that shares a particular view of faith. These kinds of verbal and visual symbols can create identity among members, advertise presence to potential members, and reassure current members that they are part of a particular grouping.

But these badges or symbols can serve a much greater purpose than forming a means of identity or even creating a sense of identification with the product or group. The symbol evokes the values of the thing that it represents. So strong is this association between the values of the organization and the symbols that represent it that the organization itself need not intervene in that relationship. The symbols evoke the values directly, without the need to visit the organization. The symbol for McDonald's burger bars, for example, evokes a strong sense of the values of that organization – burgers and chips, fast food, standards of preparation, the 'Happy Meal' that is fast food's equivalent to Mickey Mouse – that all children both recognize and relate to. Guinness has its own strong branding, as does Nike. These brand images don't just happen. Many millions of pounds are spent by the organizations to create a specific linkage between a set of values and the symbols that represent them. Marketing and branding experts work long and hard to understand the culture that the various brands have to work within, because they know only too well that brands don't operate in a vacuum – there is an interplay between the values of the culture and the values of the brand.

So the first thing that any marketing organization undertakes when it is looking at building a brand image is research. Careful, expensive and well-documented research is carried out to discover the underlying meta-narrative of the culture or cultures in which the brand has to operate. I once attended a UK briefing by the worldwide advertising agency Foote, Cone and Belding (FCB), and was presented with the meta-narrative of the culture in one striking statement: 'snuggle in the nest'. This was what most of the population were doing, according to FCB. This was their priority. This was the thing that they were spending their time, their energy and their money on. Their research, hugely expensive and paid for by their clients, had led them to this one striking conclusion. The vast majority of middle England was engaged in a nesting process. They were 'snuggling in the nest', and any product or service that helped them would sell.

Once this kind of data is gathered, analysed and accepted, further specific research is carried out to find images and stories that will work within that culture to link the symbol, or logo, with the values that the organization wishes to promote. It is no good just relying on one or two universal stories. Each culture, or sub-culture, has its own meta-narrative, and the stories that convey the values need to be carefully constructed so that they work within that meta-narrative to convey the precise feelings, emotions, values and drivers that the marketing people want.

We are, simply and frankly, talking about advertising. The great advantage of advertising over any other medium of communication is that of control. You can control the message. You can control the medium. You can control (more or less) the audience to which you are directing the advertising. And you can control the timing. The role of advertising in building the values of a brand is central to its identification and therefore to its sales. Take, for instance, a brand of perfume. The decision is made to create an Italian rural identity. Research is done amongst the target audience in the target country to discover the kind of values and images that will evoke the required response. The pictures and stories that help to create the brand image are carefully chosen to reflect the values that the marketing people have found through research that their target audience respond well to. They will then try by the extensive use of advertising to create a brand image that will associate those values and visual images with the perfume. The advertising profile may, for example, include a thirty-second television ad showing pictures of a young Italian girl harvesting flowers, in a setting that is evocative of strong rural scents and warm sunshine because this is what research has shown the target audience think of when the words 'Italian' and 'rural' are used. There will probably be a heavy overtone of sexuality – maybe the hint of a sexual relationship in the background, but not more than a hint (because the research has shown that the target audience will buy the product in order to help enhance their own sexuality) – and the pictures may also show a strong independence in the female characterization (because the background research has shown that women in the target group of that culture value strong independence for themselves!). And so the symbol for that perfume is artificially linked in the minds of the target audience, through the extensive use of research, with the values that the marketing folk think will sell the product. When you buy the product, you are buying the rural scene, the images and mythology of the advertising symbols. You are buying the advertisement. You are not buying the reality!

The reality, of course, is different. The perfume is probably chemically manufactured from its base ingredients in a grim factory in the industrial heart of a provincial city, where the nearest tree is in a park some half a mile away, where the air is polluted with carcinogens, and where the originators of the perfume are a professional team of people who work under contract for a host of different perfume houses and who have only been to Italy to spend their bonus from the last job. But does the target audience know this? Well, if they think about the product for more than a few seconds, they might guess. But they will never be shown. And the advertisements will certainly not tell them. What they will buy is not the chemical product of some grim, grey factory, but the essence of the Italian countryside. The branding of the product will have worked when sufficient numbers of people associate the symbol, or logo, of that product with the scenes of the Italian countryside produced by the advertisers.

But branding isn't an optional extra. All symbols have their brand images attached, either accidentally or through deliberate creation. The Church of England has a brand image, despite a deliberate attempt to avoid spending any money on it. If you don't attend to your brand image, then a mixture of fantasy, received wisdom and partial experience will fill the vacuum. People will think they know about your organization, but what they know will be partial, probably at least twenty years or more out of date, and almost certainly inaccurate. It is a salutary exercise to sit down with a group of people and show them some of the symbols associated with the institutional church. The Church of England tried this around the time of the millennium, and made some interesting and unwelcome discoveries. There is no doubt that the institutional churches need to do a considerable amount of work to reinvest in their brand images. Values such as 'out of touch', 'outdated', 'unscientific', 'homophobic', 'ultra-conservative' and 'anti-women' are not likely to promote membership of the Christian Church to a large section of the Church's intended target audience.

Of course, there are issues of honesty and integrity here. The Church cannot simply create whatever brand image it wishes while leaving the reality to look after itself. It has to change the reality first. The problem is, of course, that the churches have made considerable progress in addressing some of the negative values experienced by members and visitors alike; but they have done almost nothing to promote those changes among either their membership or their target audience. The retiring Archbishop of Canterbury, George Carey, seemed to recognize this towards the end of his ministry, because one would often hear him speaking most positively (what the marketing folk would call 'talking up the product') about the progress made by the Church of England.

The most fundamental question of all is that of product identity. A Mars Bar is a Mars Bar is a Mars Bar. But each church congregation is as different from all the others as it is possible to be. The liturgy may create some similarity between congregations that share the same denominational label, but there are likely to be more differences than similarities. The welcome you receive will vary from place to place, as will the quality of the coffee after the service! I have long argued, when faced with this problem by marketing experts, that as far as the Church of England is concerned, the variety of the 'product' is one of its strongest selling points. After all, where else can you go to find a community of real people, struggling with real issues, and learning to relate to one another and to God in a real setting? Where else can you have a real conversation that is not constrained by time (as with your general practitioner) or branding (try talking about Ford in a Volvo dealership) or the marketing department's agenda (the vicar is unlikely to steer you towards special offers in church this Sunday!). This is a real community, doing real things, that you can engage with on your own terms whenever you wish. It is free at the point of delivery (well, the collection plate is scarcely a 'hard sell'). And if you really can't get on with the vicar, or find the incense too strong, or dislike the 'happy clappy' atmosphere, you can go to the next church along the road and find something completely, utterly and refreshingly different. What a unique sales point!

But the kinds of symbols that are important to people who belong by association are not those of the institutional church. The brand images of the institutions, variable in their reception, are not designed to attract associate members into participation. The symbols that are important to those who belong by association are those that relate directly to the Christian faith itself, rather than to those institutions that support it. First and foremost among those symbols is the cross. Yet, along with the word 'Christian', the meaning of this symbol of the Christian faith has been devalued. Countless people wear the symbol as a kind of religious talisman, not really recognizing its meaning as the central instrument of both suffering and salvation. But there are many other Christian symbols, some of which are limited to particular geographical locations or cultural groups, that are at least as important, if not more important, in conveying the stories of the Christian faith. One of the biggest tasks facing the Church, if it is to connect with those who belong by association, is to reinvest the symbols of Christianity with their meaning.

These symbols may have originated in customs developed hundreds of years ago, and have passed into popular (if local) culture. For example, a symbol associated with Good Friday in England is the hot cross bun. These were originally baked only on Good Friday, to give to children to help convey the meaning of the death and resurrection of Jesus. The spicy sweet buns have a white cross on the top to symbolize the death of Jesus on the cross. The aromatic spices remind us of the spices with which he was buried, and the fruit reminds us of the love he has for us. The bun is baked in the shape of the stone that was rolled away from the entrance to the tomb, and the fact that they are given away to children reminds us of the free gift of salvation that is available to all of us through the death and resurrection of our Lord and Saviour. As a teaching aid, they are quite brilliant. The recipe for a good hot cross bun is highly valued, and they are immortalized in the eighteenth-century nursery rhyme:

> Hot cross buns,
> Hot cross buns,
> One a penny, two a penny,
> Hot cross buns.

This potent symbol of the Good Friday story has been used for at least two hundred years, if not longer, in punctuating the year with the story of the cross. Unlike many of the symbols of Easter Day, this symbol of Good Friday has a high 'sales rating'. It is attractive, different, tasty and evokes the days of our grandparents and great-grandparents. It echoes tradition, but is easy to bake and cheap. In other words, it is an excellent food for the marketing folk. And the result? Nearly every supermarket in the country sells them all year round, thus ruining the essential link between the hot cross bun and the events of Good Friday. What's more, the buns are sold without any explanation on the label of the meaning of the symbolism. The supermarkets are highly resistant to any link between the hot cross bun and its religious symbolism because they fear that such linkage will reduce sales amongst the (supposedly) vast majority who are sensibly secular. They think that those Christians who know the symbolism will buy them and gain an extra dimension to their purchase, while those who are agnostics, atheists or members of a non-Christian religion will be put off buying them if the symbolism is explicit. The fact that this use of a religious icon could be seen as the equivalent of robbery from the Church of some of its most meaningful symbols has escaped their notice. The problem is not the fact that they sell them, but the fact that by selling them all year round they have broken the essential link between the hot cross bun and Good Friday, the traditional day on which they were eaten.

Many churches have begun to recognize this, and have started using the hot cross bun as the central symbol in their Good Friday liturgy for children. I remember in the early 1980s asking my local baker to provide me with a couple of trays of freshly baked hot cross buns for my Good Friday service. I used them to teach the story, developing the symbolism, and then gave them away to the children and their parents. The service was not only highly successful (giving food to children is usually a success), but more importantly it was reinvesting the symbol with its original meaning.

It is this process of identification of suitable symbols, and an active programme by the churches to reinvest them with the Christian meaning, that can be one of the most potent ways of reconnecting people with their Christian faith. This is one area of mission that can have a direct impact on the understanding of the Christian faith by people who belong by association. In the case of the hot cross bun, their use in Church on Good Friday by sufficient numbers of churches will begin the process of reinvesting this particular symbol with its meaning. But there are other ways that the Church can engage with this process, not least in working with the stores that sell them to encourage them to include a slip explaining their meaning. This 'added value' approach is likely, if properly and professionally undertaken, to have considerable impact simply because of the stores' huge volumes of sales, and their wide reach.

The example of the hot cross bun may be a small and relatively trivial example of a culturally related public symbol of our faith, but it raises interesting possibilities for the future. Once the Church recognizes the role that public symbols can play in informing and developing the faith of those who belong by association, there is at least a chance that it might begin to develop a programme of action that will reinvest many more of the existing symbols with their meaning, and encourage the development of other symbols that can convey aspects of the faith that we have neglected. Often these things happen by a process of serendipity; the development, for example, of the Harvest Festival service in the middle of the nineteenth century has helped to restore the Christian Church's links with creation theology, and with farming and rural life. While it may now seem a little dated, with overtones of Victorian spirituality, it too has provided the Church with a public symbol that conveys a tremendously important aspect of our faith.

It may be clear from the discussion so far that I believe fairly strongly that the Church has a great deal of work to do in readjusting its thinking so as to value those public symbols that are in common currency, and continually to reinvest them with their meaning. Through the use of school assemblies, articles and projects in the media, 'added value' work with national retail outlets, and in many other ways, the Church can once again use these potent symbols to develop a branding that no longer relies on perception of the institution, but on the nature of the faith itself. One such attempt by the Churches' Advertising Network during the 1990s, through the use of advertising posters created by Christians working in the advertising media, produced some sparkling results. The problem for the Network, as well as the churches, was that the institutional Church refused to support the work, and it was left unguided and without resources. This fear of using the skills of the marketing and advertising world will have to be overcome if we are to learn to use the full range of the gifts and abilities of our members in the service of the Kingdom.

But public symbols are very often related to private rituals, and these private rituals are extremely important in maintaining and developing the faith of those who belong by association. A ritual is any action or group of actions and words that is repeatable and repeated to mark a particular event. For example, the singing of 'Happy Birthday to you' on someone's birthday is both a private and a public ritual, and is often linked with the symbol of the birthday cake. Rituals give meaning to events, and provide a shared framework in which the meaning of the event can be reaffirmed. These rituals convey meaning, but they also convey importance. We mark the importance of the birthday by the singing of the ritual song, by sharing in a ritual meal (often in the form of a birthday cake – or, in my office, a plate of biscuits), and by drinking a ritual drink (as in 'it's your birthday – we'll buy you a drink!').

There are a whole range of Christian rituals that are common currency in our society. They too mark importance, convey meaning and bring people together. Many of them cross the boundary of the Church and become the property of the community rather than the congregation. For example, the response 'Bless you' to a sneeze is clearly a ritual of blessing and protection, and it dates from the time of the plague, when a sneeze was often the first sign of serious illness. Rites of passage are highly important as well, but precisely because they live in two places and form a bridge between them, they are often the subject of controversy within the Church, and sometimes of conflict between the Church and the community.

One example is the public and private ritual of baptism, of utmost importance to those of us who take seriously the faith of those who belong by association. It is a good example of a ritual that belongs in two places. The Church quite rightly claims ownership of baptism, because it originated with the Church, and is its single most important statement of Christian belief and commitment. But while the ritual might belong to the Church, the act of commitment that it conveys is not the property of the Church, but of those who make that commitment. Because we live in a world where people are free to make a commitment to God on their own terms, and quite often without much thought about active participation in the congregational life of the Church, they seek to use the rituals of baptism to provide a framework for that commitment. They come to the church for the ritual, but on their own terms, because they quite rightly believe that their commitment is just that – their own! Of course, the Church can and does provide a benchmark against which to test both the orthodoxy and the level of that commitment. And that benchmark will vary from institution to institution, and very often between individual congregations and ministers. But the application of the benchmark should rarely if ever lead to rejection; rather, it should be an opportunity to continue the process of the investment of meaning into the ritual and its symbols that are owned both by the Church and by the individuals making the commitment. That dual ownership may result in very different meanings. The Church may mean one thing by baptism, and the people making the statement of commitment may mean another. Very often, families are unable to articulate the meaning of the ritual beyond its simplest application: 'We'd like our baby "done", Vicar'. Some may wince on hearing such a request, but we must not judge the commitment behind the request on the basis of an understanding of its meaning. Our Lord's words are highly appropriate here: 'Judge not, that ye be not judged' (Matthew 7.1 AV). The commitment may indeed be uninformed, but that does not diminish its strength, and the Church needs to beware of falling once again into the heresy of salvation by correct doctrine.

The form of the ritual may vary enormously from community to community. Some may have more than a hint of pagan practice – the well-dressing that is popular in the West Country, for example, could well be a direct throwback to the pagan worship of the spirits of the place – but they all provide a marvellous opportunity for the Church to invest meaning into public rituals that inform the beliefs of the communities that practise them. The nature of that investment needs to be thought through fairly carefully. For example, it is always helpful to allow the local media to cover a public ritual, and to provide an explanation of some of the aspects of that ritual in a way that reinforces the Christian teaching or content. And many journalists are more than happy to respond to this, because it often comes as a personal surprise to them to discover that such and such a ritual has a deeper meaning. Following the local calendar, and spotting these public rituals in advance, giving a short statement to the media on their meaning, can result in an in-depth interview seen or heard by many thousands of people. This kind of teaching, which is highly visual and almost completely detached from the religious ceremonies that take place Sunday by Sunday in the local church, can speak directly to those who belong by association, and can considerably raise their understanding of the particular aspect of Christian teaching attached to the ritual. What the Church has to learn is that these rituals, which on the surface seem so detached from contemporary liturgical practice, are themselves a kind of liturgy, but one that belongs not to the Church but to the local community. To take one's place alongside the local community, helping it to understand its own liturgy more deeply, is a highly satisfying process.

Not all rituals are public. It would be interesting to discover (and almost certainly the statistic exists somewhere) how many families say some kind of grace before a family meal. It is certainly the practice in many dining clubs, Rotary meetings, Masonic lodge meetings, and many other institutions, to say grace before a formal dinner. This ritual acknowledgement would benefit from considerably more teaching than it is given in churches in the UK. But why stop at grace? There are countless opportunities for the Church to develop rituals of the home that will, in time, spread and inform the faith of those who have stopped participating in congregational worship, or who come across family traditions through marriage or friendship. Is there, for example, a ritual for the burial of a family pet? Most children grieve deeply over the death of an animal, especially one that has been in their care, and this grieving forms part of the learning process. Many will wish to find a small corner of the garden for a burial, and that burial is almost universally accompanied by a ritual that echoes the commendation of most funeral services, whether or not that commendation is more than a simple spoken 'goodbye'. Rituals for the planting of a tree, or the laying of a new garden path, can echo the ritual of the blessing of a house. To make known to a local community that the church is more than willing to offer such rituals, or better still, to develop and publish them in local community magazines, can provide the implicit

131

permission needed for families to do these kinds of things themselves, as well as developing a sense of the religious dimension to the various small but significant moments of family life.

These moments of private ritual can also become a bridge to understanding the public liturgy of the Christian community. To take part in a small ritual for the burial of a family pet can provide the link to taking part in the bigger ritual for the funeral service or the eucharist. The ritual for the blessing of a house can provide a bridge to the blessing of a marriage, or the baptism of a child. And there are many other ways in which the development of small rituals can also help participant members of the church understand that the acknowledgement of the sacred can be done just as well outside the church building as within it. As I have argued elsewhere in this book, the central acts of Christian witness – baptism, Eucharist, penitence, daily prayer – all can be celebrated just as easily within the home as within the church, and sometimes much more effectively.

Chapter 11

Christendom is Dead: Long Live Christianity!

━━━━━

If you talk long enough and carefully enough to people who believe but don't belong, one of the emerging points of commonality is their dislike of organizations based on authority, with all its inevitable consequences of the exercise of power, and their preference for networks based on shared energy where they are free to explore ideas of both faith and practice. Many share a love of task-centred or ideas-centred groups, and a dislike of institutions. Perhaps surprisingly, this same dislike is also found in many of us who belong by participation. The discovery of networks based on shared energy – the energy, for example, that is generated in developing a group to house the homeless, or to meet with people of other faiths – can transform a Christian faith that is largely duty-based into a faith that is revitalized.

The use of the word 'Christendom' as a pejorative term for certain forms of structural Christianity is an interesting one, and one that is growing among both theologians and lay Christians. 'Christendom' has meant many things, from the geographical area where Christianity was the dominant religion, to the places where Christian faith and national politics combined to create a form of Christian imperialism. Unfortunately, much of today's formal expression of Christianity, both in the Anglican Church (and particularly in the concept of the Anglican Communion), and in the Catholic and, to a lesser extent, in the Orthodox Churches, continues to reflect a form of Christian imperialism that has come down to us directly from the days of 'Christendom'. The word describes a kind of superior authority that is experienced in the imposition of forms of organization, worship and belief on its members as well as the local communities in which it exists, an imposition that sits uncomfortably with a religion of the cross and the incarnation. For a very large number of people who reject organized religion, it is imperialism that is rejected, and not Christianity itself.

The story of the temptation of Jesus tells of Jesus being offered all the kingdoms of the world. It was secular power that was being offered, and Jesus utterly rejects the embrace of secular power as a way of evangelizing. Yet too often the Church has embraced secular power. In every case, it has harmed its mission. If you accept the proposition that Christianity needs to break free of its remaining links with Roman or British imperialism, then maybe the most urgent task facing most institutional forms of western Christianity is the task of transformation from an essentially imperialist institution that has lost its ability to relate to people who belong by association into a movement that can captivate them and engage their energies and vision through its concentration on energy-based, rather than power-based, structures.

The task is not an easy one, not only because the latent imperialism of the Anglican Church is still a part of our British culture, and therefore difficult to recognize, but also because it requires a reversal of the normal process of development. Most institutions begin life as a movement, a seminal idea or philosophy that gains adherents and slowly develops a structure for the transmission and development of the original idea or philosophy. Christianity was, in its origins, little different. The history of the early Church is the story of just such a movement. It developed from the frightened first twelve disciples into an underground movement that made even the powerful Roman emperors feel threatened. That underground movement grew in credibility, size and authority, and with the conversion of the ruling classes it became the leading faith of the Empire. As such, the structures that it had developed to support itself as a movement changed and became more inflexible. It developed from a movement into an institution.

Christians have, of course, understood that development from the moment of the first Pentecost as one driven by the Spirit of God, a development that was and is far from random, and powered by more than an idea or philosophy. The Christian movement, like all movements, grew structures that suited its purpose. Those structures were originally geared towards the transmission of the Christian faith and the development and maintenance of orthodoxy in a culture where the penalties adhering to a religion that claimed a higher authority than the emperor were considerable. In fact, the pressing need to define orthodoxy meant that the debate about who belonged, and who did not belong, to this emerging movement was strong and energizing. Orthodoxy was continually being defined and redefined as the Christian faith met with ideas and expressions that did not fully reflect the experience and the teaching of the Apostles. The debates were lively, heated and sometimes fierce. But above all, they were part of the day-to-day dialogue between Christians, not conducted at some higher level that didn't touch them.

The characteristics of a movement in its early stages are, first of all, a strong identification with the small group of leaders who brought the movement into existence, and a clear and simple purpose. For the early Church, this identification was with the person of Jesus, experienced through a clear association with the Apostles. The Pauline epistles show all too clearly the way in which the early Christian movement found its identity in relation to that small group of leaders. Paul assumes responsibility, along with a small group of Apostles, for a sizeable number of Christians spread across a wide area. Peter writes to two groups of Christians – a group that clearly draw their identity from their Jewish background, and a group that is identified much more with the Gentile community. The author of the letter to the Hebrews draws on a Jewish background to encourage that particular section of the Church to continue its Christian orthodoxy. But despite their great diversity, all of them demonstrate this one simple principle – that of identification with a small group of leaders intent on developing and maintaining a movement that is formed around the experience of Jesus' resurrection and teaching, empowered by the Spirit of God.

And so, in its early stages, Christianity was highly successful. The debate about orthodoxy, who was 'in' and who was 'out', was a very strong force in developing structures that slowly, but surely, turned the Church into an institution, with its own hierarchy and its own pastoral and theological structures.

As for purpose, this was breathtaking in its scope: to proclaim the rule and authority of God as experienced and demonstrated in Jesus regardless of national or, eventually, racial boundaries, and to bring all the nations of the world into Christian discipleship. It is easy for us today to forget that this aim really was revolutionary, not only in historical but also in theological terms. In pagan communities, most gods were local gods, related to particular places, and with a geographically limited sphere of influence. If you visited a different place or a different community, you often needed to acknowledge the gods of that place, bringing offerings and seeking to discover ways of behaviour which the local gods would approve. The idea of a God who could be worshipped regardless of place and racial group, and whose ethical code was global in its application, was a new idea to most, even to those Jews who already accepted a global vision encapsulated by some of their later prophets. This new idea of the one God made present in the person of Jesus, and claiming universal authority and allegiance, formed around it a new structure whose main purpose was the transmission of this global faith and the maintenance of a global orthodoxy. It is a fact of history, and probably inevitable given fallen human nature, that the global orthodoxy that was (and is) so highly prized and so much sought after contains within itself the seeds of its own fragmentation. But part of the reason for this fragmentation was because of the institutionalization of the Church. The Christian movement continued to evolve, and very quickly became not a movement based on energy, but an institution based on power with members enough to rival the Roman Empire, and the politics to match.

And so Christianity moved from founder to early movement with a small group of leaders, and from early movement to the classic definition of a movement, and then, inevitably, onwards to becoming an institution. Despite some fragmentation along the way, the Christian Church has remained largely an institutional church – or at least, a group of institutions – with all the solidity and survivability of an institution, but with many of its problems as well, chief of which, as with any institution, is a loss of identification with the original founders and, consequently, a loss of the initial sense of purpose. Fifteen hundred years or so after first gaining its full sense of institution, the Church – at least in western Christianity – is in crisis, not because it has lost its faith, but because in a rapidly changing culture, it needs to transform itself in reverse, as it were, from its institutional form back into a movement once more. Yet perhaps the use of the word 'back' is misleading, because it implies a reversal, as if we are trying to discover and re-create the past. But the process I am trying to describe is perhaps better understood as a form of de-institutionalization – not a reversal, but an evolutionary process.

The key to this transformation is the movement from a Church based on power structures to a Church based on energy structures. The key to understanding an institution is to understand how, and where, power is exercised. Within the typical diocese, power resides with the bishop. The advent of synodical government was an attempt to move power away from the bishop to a more broadly based government that includes lay people; however, no episcopal system can cope with the definition of doctrine by democracy, and so there is always a tension within a synodically governed church that has to do with the maintenance of orthodoxy. The Church has traditionally seen the definition of orthodoxy as a task of the bishops, meeting together to study, to pray and to decide. The exercise of power, particularly when it comes to the definition and maintenance of orthodoxy, is expressed in authority, and authority is often received by the clergy and the laity in terms of permission. Thus one of the hallmarks of an institutional church is the way in which the clergy and laity seek to define the practice of their faith in terms of permission, or those things that we are (or more often are not) allowed to do or to believe.

It is this sense of permission that leads to the tyranny of the 'ought' that pervades an institutionalized church. All too frequently we come across people who are doing things not because they have the energy to do them – in fact, they often wonder why they are doing them at all – but because they have joined a system that was doing them, and they believe that the practice of their faith demands that they go on doing them. Christianity is confused with the maintenance of an institution. If the ritual has no meaning, or has lost its meaning, continuing it becomes a drain on energy rather than an energizer. In these circumstances, we do things not because we want to, because we have energy for them, but because we believe that this is how we 'ought' to do them. We feel the systemic pressure to work within the permissions that we or our forebears have received, rather than do the things that we have the energy and very probably the vision to do. We seek to make our belief system work along 'authorized' lines, rather than explore those beliefs that excite or energize us. And so we substitute the 'ought' for dynamic, living faith. The tyranny of the 'ought' is the negative side of a church based on the exercise of power, and the result of a church dominated by a sense of restriction is that belonging becomes a substitute for believing. Ultimately, the Church is experienced by newcomers as people doing things because they feel they 'ought' to do them, and believing things because they feel they 'ought' to believe them. It is not experienced as a dynamic community driven by people who are doing things because they believe they are important, or believing things because this is what makes ultimate sense to them. This kind of church – one based on power rather than energy – is attractive only to those who need security. It is a hospital, not a church; it is not a place for risk-takers, and it is systemically opposed to risk. It becomes a place of hidebound conservatism and empty ritual. No wonder that the Church increasingly fails to attract the young, who are attracted by energy systems rather than power systems, and risk rather than safety. As we shall see later, one answer to the problem of loss of understanding of a behaviour, or loss of energy to continue it, is to explain the meaning behind the behaviour, and thus reinvest the ritual or symbol with its original meaning. Another is to create a new and more effective meaning for the same task or ritual. This certainly can transform the energy level of the person undertaking the task, or performing the ritual. But where this cannot be done, an enormous amount of energy can be released by giving permission to stop doing whatever it is, and to refocus on something for which the person or group do have real energy.

The key to transforming the Church from its decaying institutionaliza-tion to a more dynamic 'movement' is in changing our responses from those of power – or more particularly, from the negative side of power which is experienced in terms of 'ought' – to those of energy. We need to learn to value those spiritual energies that drive us to question why things are done 'that way' rather than the way that makes more sense to us. We need to recognize the desire to stop doing something that has, frankly, lost meaning for us as a good desire, not a loss of faith. There is an argument that it is good for us to go through the ritual performance of something while having only a vague understanding of the meaning behind the ritual. This can be a way of learning, but it is valid only up to a point, and usually only for someone who understands why they are being asked to undertake a ritual which they don't fully understand. But most often, we continue to require people to do things for which they have little energy and less understanding. Why continue to do something just because it has always been done, if none of us have any energy for doing it that way and would seriously like to try different things done in different ways? Would it not be better to allow a church simply to stop doing all those things that it does merely because it feels it 'ought' to do them, and to liberate it to coalesce around those things that it has energy for? Is our theology of the Holy Spirit not sufficient to allow us to believe that he really will lead us into all truth?

The way to achieve this kind of transformation is not to evade the in-stitutional church, but to enter it fully; to immerse oneself in its form, and to try to 'read back' from those forms and structures the real purpose for their original construction. Are those purposes essentially gospel pur-poses, or are they cultural adaptations, put in place in order to allow the gospel to become incarnate in a particular culture at a particular time? If they are cultural – and the vast majority are – then it is perfectly legitimate to seek to re-express those purposes in different ways. Often it will be in ways that at first sight bear little relationship to the original form or struc-ture. Very often, in this process one discovers the original task that the structures were there to achieve. And so the task, provided it is relevant to the gospel of the cross, can be redefined and achieved in ways very dif-ferent from the way that the original structure envisaged.

A good, if minor, example of this kind of 'reading back' from a struc-ture is the development of the giving of the peace during the eucharist. For many people, its reintroduction seemed both arbitrary and intrusive. 'Why do we have to shake hands with our neighbour?' It was a distinctly un-British thing to do even though it used a distinctly British symbol. So why was it there? Why did the early Church have such a thing? The 'kiss of peace' was more than a handshake. But heaven forbid that I should be asked to kiss my neighbour; shaking his hand is bad enough. This custom drove many people to question it, and in questioning the purpose, there was in some churches a 'reading back' of the original purpose. Jesus' words about making peace with my neighbour before bringing my gift to the altar were made starkly visible in the symbolism, and this has led to a much greater awareness of the need for communal 'peace', and for the healing of poisoned or broken relationships within many Christian communities.

But there are many other ways of 'reading back' from the structures. For example, the simple regularity of the offices on which matins and even-song are based can lead to a much more focused daily discipline in our own prayer lives, as we discover the real purpose behind the daily offices – that they are a school of prayer, and a useful discipline to teach us to pray. And so on.

Thus a church based on energy rather than power will be heavily task-centred. The energy of its members will be released into achieving the tasks that the original structures were created to achieve. And because there will be much more clarity about the tasks that are to engage the energy of the church, there will be a much stronger identification with those tasks by the members of the church. No longer will they have the feeling that they are merely serving the institution by repeating rituals they do not understand; they will begin to feel that they are part of a church that is serving the Kingdom of God through an active and enga-ging programme, even if that active and engaging programme is focused on being holy, rather than doing holy things.

I found a classic example of how such a refocusing can work out in prac-tice in a meeting with a Muslim woman. She had worked in education for a number of years, having gained her degree at a secular university. Her faith as a Muslim was not merely intact, but strong. But in the process of learn-ing her faith, she had also learned to distinguish between those things in the received practice of her faith that were culture-bound and those things that were intrinsic to Islam itself, regardless of its cultural context. She sat lightly – very lightly indeed – to those things that were culture-bound, but developed those things that she believed were intrinsic to the faith of Islam. The result was that her faith looked less and less like the Islam that her parents had received. She no longer wore the traditional clothing of a Muslim woman. She was single, yet she worked outside the home. Her parents experienced her practice as un-Islamic. For her part, she found it more and more difficult to take part in what she increasingly saw as a litera-list interpretation of a faith that was not so much based on the Qur'an as on a culturally specific version of Islam that was no longer relevant even to the culture in which it had originated. The family had moved from Iraq to the UK many years ago, and had brought with them, and continued to practise, precisely the form of Islam they had been practising at the time they left Iraq. Because of her education, this woman had travelled on a number of occasions back to Iraq and realized that the version of Islam that her parents were still practising seemed very old-fashioned indeed to contemporary Iraqi Muslims.

To stop doing or believing those things that we do or believe because we feel we 'ought', rather than because we believe they are central to our faith, can result in a new form of faith that is focused clearly on our core beliefs, but which can distance us from others, and can make it hard for us to fit into the established practice of our religion. But it can also liberate others who have felt alienated from faith because they were, and are, unable to accept a version of the faith that is expressed in terms of a culture or belief system that is outdated and inadequate.

One area where this refocusing of understanding can have a major impact is in the area of faith and science. Students often claim that it is impossible to be a Christian and a scientist because they have inherited, sometimes from their parents, sometimes from teachers, the view that Christianity conflicts directly with science. Science demands proof, and there can be no proof of Christianity. And Christians believe in the Bible, which teaches that God made the world in seven days, which science has disproved. Therefore Christianity and science are incompatible. Some students, who wish to hold to their Christian faith, end up rejecting science; others, who wish to be true to their intellect, end up rejecting Christianity. Yet an exploration of the views with which they feel uncomfortable can result in a surprising release of energy. For, of course, science is not just about facts, and Christian faith is not about believing, like the White Queen, six impossible things before breakfast. There are many things that scientists take as fact that are impossible to prove, but that can reasonably be deduced from the scientific evidence. That does not stop them looking for proof, of course, but it would be a bold scientist who rejected everything that could not be categorically demonstrated. Christians, too, do not believe things simply because someone – or something – asks them to. They carefully weigh the evidence. Often their personal religious experience supports the other evidence for God. But that is a very different thing from simply screwing up the courage to believe things that science suggests are impossible. If there is a God, then he gave us a brain and expects us to use it. For this reason, there are many things that Christians have stopped believing because the evidence for them no longer measures up. Few Christians today believe that God created the world in seven days. This might have been a satisfactory belief for cultures who had very little in the way of scientific method, but it is entirely inadequate for contemporary Christianity, unless Christians are prepared to reject the foundations of geology and archaeology (together with biology, astronomy, physics and just about every other scientific discipline) as a giant conspiracy!

In the same way that we are able to embrace a developmental understanding of our faith, we need to be willing to embrace a developmental understanding of the structures and forms that allow that faith to be practised. The way we have traditionally structured our worship may be very useful in a rural culture or a Benedictine community, but it may make participation impossible for an increasing number of people in our contemporary society. So to hang on to the structures that shape our worship in the face of obvious change is slowly to turn us into people whose main task is to support an inherited institution, rather than a living faith.

I said at the start of this chapter that one of the commonalities among those who belong by association rather than participation is their dislike of organizations based on authority, with all the inevitable consequences of the exercise of power, and their preference for networks based on shared energy where they are free to explore ideas of both faith and practice. For many people brought up in an institutional church, this sounds too dangerous an option. After all, if people are free to explore ideas of both faith and practice, then they are free to leave orthodoxy for any kind of self-defined religion. But it is precisely in this freedom that two key elements of our faith begin to come together, and it is precisely this kind of freedom that will engage the hearts and minds of those who feel that 'organized religion' is too organized, too restrictive, for them. The first is the gospel statement that the task of the Holy Spirit is to lead us into all truth (John 16.13). Anyone who begins an honest exploration of the Christian faith is not alone in the process. It may be a scary concept, but it is none the less central to our understanding of God, that whenever we make a serious exploration into faith (and the question of which faith is deliberately left open) the Holy Spirit is present with us, nurturing us, prompting us, guiding us, so that our pilgrimage takes us closer and closer to God himself. And besides, is safety, even safe orthodoxy, necessarily the aim of Christian faith? Isn't the risk of exploring the full dimensions of any possible relationship with the sacred, with the one we Christians know as God, infinitely preferable to gritting our teeth and staying within the confines of a doctrinal orthodoxy that neither excites us nor meets our needs? I suspect that the risk of exploring the full dimensions of such a relationship will in any event be mitigated by the Holy Spirit's quiet voice of caution if we contemplate stepping into places that will cause us harm. After all, a loving God is hardly likely to give us the freedom to explore life in all its fullness, and the assurance of the guidance of the Holy Spirit, and then abandon us to our fate should we take the invitation too seriously.

The second is quite simply that God has given us a brain, he has given us freedom, and he expects us to use both of these gifts in the development of an understanding of himself and in the relationships we develop with him and with each other. It is a mark of mature Christian faith that it encourages people to develop their own individuality, their own special gifts and abilities, and to become as fully as possible the unique person that God has created. And that can't be done by forcing people into a predetermined shape, or setting out boundaries that, if crossed, lead to rejection. There is nothing quite so suffocating as a religion that wishes to create clones. People are stifled, fear is generated, and gifts and abilities are renounced or rejected, simply because a religion tries to force people into a narrow track that is simply a desire for conformity, rather than a celebration of orthodoxy. Real, full-blooded Christianity is not like this. It is a faith that is prepared not only to take risks, but to support the risk-takers. In fact, being able to take risks for God is itself a strong form of faith, or trust, in the God who will stand by us as we learn and grow. It is often the rejection of a narrow, conformist experience of Christianity that leads people away from participation into association. If the Church can celebrate their pilgrimage, provide rituals and symbols for them that will help them find anchor points for that pilgrimage, and support them through whatever process of learning or exploration their individual path requires, then it will have done a very great deal to restore some of the connections with those who belong by association that we have lost through our insistence on orthodoxy at all costs in both belief and practice.

Chapter 12

Conclusion

At the heart of this book has been an exploration into the hypothesis that believing is the strongest and most important form of belonging. At first sight, this doesn't seem to need much argument. 'He who believes in me', claims Jesus in John's gospel, 'has eternal life' (John 6.47 RSV). Despite the attempt by some of our churches to change this claim to mean 'He who goes to my church has eternal life', the genie keeps escaping from the bottle. However, Christians have continued to test belief by belonging – particularly belonging to a local Christian congregation. The result of this thinking has been to dismiss those who claim faith in Christ, but who do not participate at least fairly regularly in church worship, as at best 'fringe' members, and at worst, non-believers. Yet I have argued, I hope reasonably convincingly, that just as there are those who belong by participation, there are also many who believe but don't belong. I have called them 'associate' members – those who belong by association. They might once have been participant members but have left participant membership for a variety of reasons: dissatisfaction with the church's application of faith, moving away from the neighbourhood of the church, an argument with the vicar or congregation, or simply a change of spiritual landscape that has led them slowly but inexorably away from participation. Or they may never have participated in any established or organized way. Their faith may have been formed through a natural recognition of the sacredness of creation, or of the inevitability of a loving God. They may have had their faith formed by institutions other than the church; by their school, for example, or by programmes they have watched on television. That there are many who find the whole concept of robed clergy ministering in gothic buildings repugnant is beyond argument. But it does not mean that their belief is somehow false, nor that they belong any less to the Kingdom of God. And in today's rapidly changing culture, they are likely to form an increasing proportion of the church's membership.

Yet the mainstream denominations confine their ministry almost entirely to their participant congregations. Success is measured by calculating the number of bottoms on pews (even though this is often denied). The Church of England recently changed its basic method of counting, but then concentrated its new methodology exclusively on those who attend worship – on its participant members. It might argue correctly that the old system was under-recording the numbers of people attending; what it has failed to recognize or make any attempt to count is the number of people who believe, who express a strong allegiance, but who do not belong to any particular congregation, and who have no wish to do so. The clues are all there, should anyone care to look. In one Anglican deanery, over one month, a massive 55 per cent of attendees were there only once (Holmes 2001). One might argue that they were occasional worshippers, participants who participate only infrequently. But it is much more likely that a sizeable number of them were either casual visitors exploring faith, or associate members who happened to drop in during the month of the survey. Independent surveys consistently show membership of the Church of England of at least around 50 per cent of the population, but participation at under 10 per cent. Even allowing for those whose declaration of membership is so nominal as to be unrecognizable as any kind of believing – and assuming (extremely generously) that figure to be half of those who do not attend – that still leaves a massive 20 per cent of the population who genuinely believe, but do not belong. That is double the number of people who are participant members.

Yet the churches do little to reach them, and even less to inform and educate their faith. Analysis of the way churches spend their money – always a good indication of the actual tasks they are undertaking as opposed to the words they use – shows that at least 90 per cent of their budget is spent on the 10 per cent of the population who come to church. It is a case of feeding sheep who are already fat. In missiological terms alone this is a failure. But it is a double failure not to recognize the reality of the faith of those who believe but do not belong. Not only are we doing little to nurture and support them; we are increasingly putting barriers in their way, alienating those whose spirituality is formed around sacred places that might be a long way from their homes, producing doctrinal reasons for rejecting those in whom we have completely failed to develop doctrine, and refusing ministry to those who come to us for help in developing what is often an unformed and unfocused, but very real, faith. When we do make contact, we assume that our task is to bring them into participant membership, and when they naturally resist, we either assume that we have failed, or that their faith was not real anyway.

The data are missing. While the churches are generally fairly good at researching those who are participants, and finding better and more accurate ways of counting them, they have done very little to establish the pattern of believing rather than belonging. They have simply assumed that the test of belief is belonging, and proceeded accordingly. Never ones for spending much on research anyway, what little they have spent has been on participation. The excellent efforts of people like Leslie Francis and David Hay have largely been overlooked by the mainstream churches. Attempts to create a research base, such as the recent Churches Information for Mission group, has not attracted the kind of funding it deserves.

Yet in our pubs, in our universities, in hospitals and prisons, in schools and colleges, in countless offices and factories, there are people whose lives are guided by their faith. They pray regularly, and if pressed would own allegiance to the Christian faith. They have made a choice, and the choice has been for God. For a variety of reasons, some of which we have explored, they do not find that sitting on a pew for an hour on a Sunday does much for their spiritual growth. They explore their faith as and when they can. Some will do so in quite unorthodox ways, visiting pagan or new age websites, joining Druid hearths, or simply walking quietly through the countryside recognizing the sacredness of creation. Others will 'dip into' church life, possibly visiting our cathedrals, or making a retreat at Taizé or Iona or in one of our monastic communities. Their faith may well be expressed in action during the week or the weekend, rather than in pews on a Sunday morning. Running drop-in centres for the unemployed, or working in charity shops, taking responsibility for youth work when few in the community manage to find time for young people, they find that this stretches their faith much more than membership of a local church ever did. Some who joined the churches with great expectation of becoming part of a community that could at least attempt to change society for the better found that the height of their achievement lay in reading a lesson, or being elected to deanery synods. Risk-taking based on prayer and a practical application of the gospel has too often been rejected in favour of a closed piety that has become inward-focused. So the drift continues from a church that makes too little demand, rather than too much.

The problem is likely to escalate unless we change our attitude. Disintermediation has shown us the benefits of 'going direct'. More and more people of faith will look at a church and ask 'How can this church help develop my spiritual pilgrimage?', rather than 'What can I do for the church?' Unless we can see participant membership as a means of serving the larger community of believing, we will be stuck in a continual and ultimately futile pattern of trying to bring everyone into participant membership. Our finances, geared as they are to income derived entirely from participants, will continue to decline, yet there are exciting new possibilities of funding simply by adapting our finances to embrace the needs of those who belong by association. At the same time, a mechanistic answer to a problem expressed in mechanistic terms is unlikely to satisfy anyone very much. People are longing for authentic spirituality. In order to become a truly spiritual community, the Church has to continue to divest itself of its institutional framework, and re-engage its members in a spiritual movement that more closely resembles the network of relationships that gave it birth. In our present culture this means concentrating more on our theology of creation than on our theology of salvation – or at least interpreting our doctrines of salvation in terms of the trees, the animals and the whole ecology of the planet. It will see nature as sacred, not in some pantheistic way, but as the first great incarnation implicit in the Genesis narrative. And it means moving from a faith based around communal worship for an hour a week to a faith centred on revolutionary change in the world in which we live, on its expression in the family home, in small residential communities, and at the hands of lay people rather than clergy. This is going to come hard to a church that has interpreted the cross and the resurrection almost solely in terms of salvation administered by a professional priesthood, and that has a very poor record on environmental protest. Yet implicit in the person and work of Jesus is the recognition of the sacredness of creation. It is not just the stuff of humanity that is taken on in the incarnation; it is the stuff of creation itself. God is made flesh in a world of trees, plants, animals and humans.

Most of us recognize the need for change. We have inherited patterns of worship, of church structures, that no longer excite or energize us. We continue to do it this way simply because this is what we think Christianity is. The risk of doing things differently seems too big a risk to take. And so we continue to do those things that we think ought to be done, and fail to do those things that God is calling us to do. We remain safe, protected, ineffective and unfulfilled.

But the good news of the gospel is that we can change. We can find liberating ways of walking alongside people who have a faith that is subtly different from our own, who do not wish to be confined to a denomination, or a set of pews on a Sunday morning, yet who can teach us new ways of exercising our faith. New networks are springing up, based on relationships rather than institutional structures. A group of Christians who come together to serve a local community – running a youth club on a Sunday morning, for instance, and praying for that work on a Wednesday evening – are just as much a worshipping community as any other. We have a very large community of those whose belonging is their believing. It is time we both recognized them and learned to serve them better. There is much that the Church can do to foster and nurture the faith of those whose believing is their belonging. We can use the media more effectively. We can set out a programme of reinvesting the symbols and rituals of our faith with their meaning – the symbols and rituals that are used without understanding by so many in our culture. We can seek the transformation of the local church, of the institutional church, and of the cathedral community by supporting more openly and effectively those who are prepared to take the risk of trying new ways of belonging. We can work on ways of reinvesting the family with its sacred meaning and the ritual to express that sacredness. We can begin a dialogue with pagans and others who disagree with us, and open up new pathways of understanding that will inform and enrich our own faith.

But none of this can be done without embracing and welcoming the cross. This is not merely the supreme symbol of Christian faith; it is a symbol that develops its own meaning. It is the pathway to fulfilment, to freedom from the dreadful malaise of fear that grips so much of our institutional life. To have died with Christ is to be set free from the fear of death, or of criticism, or of the loss of career. To have died to self is to be liberated to speak the truth that we feel in our bones, to give up the dreadful 'oughts' of our inherited practices, and to challenge our own and our friends' behaviour when that seems so out of touch and inappropriate. We can learn to reinvest our money not in feeding sheep that are already fat, but in providing new pastures for those who have yet to understand the meaning of the faith that they hold. The cross allows us, gives us freedom and authority, to break down the human barriers we erect and that prevent so many people from entering the liberating and joyful experience of sacred space and Christian worship.

None of this can be done without prayer. And an hour once a week is not enough. We desperately need the equivalent of the ashram, the small residential community or its equivalent, that helps us to grow to know each other and God in a relationship of honesty and compassion. By learning to live together in prayer, living the life of the cross, we can begin to model to others the way of the carpenter of Nazareth. For it is only when we have got rid of the fears, the inward-looking selfishness that turns the Church into a substitute for the golf club, that we can learn to live for others, and really to celebrate the faith of those who belong by association.

Notes and References

Notes

1 BELONGING IN AN AGE OF UNBELONGING

1 See, for example, some of the writings of the radical orthodox theologians.

3 BELONGING AND PLACE

1 For a discussion of the meaning of this verb, see von Rad (1972: 49).
2 Figures supplied to the author by the Office for National Statistics.
3 Figures supplied to the author by the Office for National Statistics.
4 Figures supplied to the author by the Office for National Statistics.

9 MEDIA AND MISSION

1 For example, in the Freeserve television advertisements broadcast during December 2000 and January 2001, depicting naked middle-aged surfers being encouraged to recapture the 'freedom' they were denied in their youth by the restrictive culture of the time.

References

Andrews, Dave (1999), *Christi-anarchy: Radical Spirituality for a New Millennium*, Oxford: Lion Publishing.
Brierley, Peter (2001), *Christian England*, London: Marc Europe.
Brinsmead, Robert (1989), *The Two Sources of Morality and Religion*, New York: Henry Holt.
Brown-Humes, Christopher (2001), 'Survey – Creative Business: Advertising and Children', *Financial Times*, 16 January 2001.
Davie, Grace (1994), *Religion in Britain since 1945*, Oxford: Blackwell.
Finney, John (1992), *Finding Faith Today: How Does It Happen?*, London: British and Foreign Bible Society.
Flood, Robert (1999), *Rethinking the Fifth Discipline*, London: Routledge.

Francis, Leslie J. (1994), *Believing Without Belonging: The Teenage Experience*, London: Unitarian Press.

Hay, David, and Hunt, Kate (2000), 'Understanding the Spirituality of People Who Don't Go to Church', a report on the findings of the Adult Spirituality Project at the University of Nottingham; available at < www.ctbi.org.uk/ ccom/documents >.

Heald, Gordon (1999), 'Taking Faith's Temperature', *The Tablet*, vol. 253, no. 8313 (18 December 1999), p. 1729.

Heald, Gordon (2001), 'The British Christmas', *The Tablet*, vol. 255, no. 8415 (22–9 December 2001), p. 1857.

Holmes, John (2001), *Church Attendance in the Deanery of Almondbury, 19th October to 7th December 2000*, Wakefield: Wakefield Diocese.

Kay, William K., and Francis, Leslie J. (1996), *Drift from the Churches: Attitude Toward Christianity During Childhood and Adolescence*, Cardiff: University of Wales Press.

Lawton, Richard (1978), *The Census and Social Structure*, London: Frank Cass.

Mass-Observation (1948), *Churchgoing: Survey of 2055 People on their Churchgoing Habits for 'Daily Graphic'*, Report 3027 (August 1948), Mass-Observation Archive, University of Sussex, Brighton.

Moore, James R. (1988) (ed.), *Religion in Victorian Britain. Volume III: Sources*, Manchester: Manchester University Press.

National Centre for Social Research (various years), *British Social Attitudes Surveys*; available from the UK Data Archive < www.data-archive.ac.uk >.

Office for National Statistics (2001a), *Abortion Statistics 2000*, Series AB No. 27, Office for National Statistics, England and Wales. Available at < www. statistics.gov.uk >.

Office for National Statistics (2001b), *Marriage, Divorce and Adoption Statistics 2000*, Series FM No. 2, Office for National Statistics, England and Wales. Available at < www.statistics.gov.uk >.

Richter, Philip J., and Francis, Leslie J. (1998), *Gone But Not Forgotten: Church Leaving and Returning*, London: Darton, Longman and Todd.

von Rad, Gerhard (1972), *Genesis*, English translation, Norwich: Fletcher & Son Ltd.

Ward, Graham (2001) (ed.), *Blackwell Companion to Modern Theology*, Oxford: Blackwell Publishers.

Index

Abraham 36, 46
Alpha Courses vi, 6, 103
Andrews, Dave 51, 53
Atwood, Karin 95

Baptist Church 15–16
belief: and belonging v, 21–3, 147;
within church doctrines 56–64;
different faith groups 19;
Durkheim's affiliation, practice,
belief 15–16; evolving 140–1;
intermediation 5–6; simplicity
and complexity 11–12; types of
63–4
belonging: associate members vi;
and believing v, 21–3, 147;
within creation 27–31; identity
through media 2–5; to Islam 60;
sacredness of place 32–6;
transitions and rituals 35–43
Benedict, St 54
Bible, the: covenant theology 45–6;
see also individual books and
gospels
Brierley, Peter 16
Brinsmead, Robert 53
British Broadcasting Corporation
(BBC) 108–9
British Social Attitudes Survey 18
Brown, Revd Brian 117, 118
Burns, Stuart 102

Carey, Archbishop George 126
cathedrals: as centres of association

98–105; and the community 80;
education 99–100
Chesterton, G. K. 65
Christianity: doctrines and
boundaries 50–1, 53, 56–64;
failure of 'participant' thinking
23–5; God and nature 33–4;
power structure of 133–8;
simplicity and complexity 11–12
church membership: and belief v;
choosing to belong 6–8; clergy
and ministers 22; covenant
theology 45–7; defining 15–16;
failure of 'participant' thinking
23–5; measuring 16–21, 88, 144;
and parish records 81–3;
participation *versus* association
vi, 7, 14–15, 20–3, 144; prodding
into participation 49; social
inclusion 12–13
Church of England: defining
members 15; General Synod 71;
House of Lords reform and 73;
image of 125–6; membership 12–
13, 19, 23; 'oughts' and 'reading
back' 138–42; as power structure
133–8; principles for
transforming 74; radical gospel
74–6; *see also* cathedrals,
churches, parish system
churches: availability 83–6; closed
sets 51–5; emotional health 59–
60; intermediation 5–6, 7, 24,
145; putting faith into action 12–